August-Wilhelm Scheer

# Architecture of Integrated Information Systems

Foundations of
Enterprise Modelling

With 160 Figures

Springer-Verlag

Berlin Heidelberg New York
London Paris Tokyo
Hong Kong Barcelona
Budapest

Professor Dr. August-Wilhelm Scheer
Director of the Institut für Wirtschaftsinformatik
and the CIM Technology Transfer Center
University of Saarland
Im Stadtwald, Gebäude 14
D-6600 Saarbrücken 11, FRG

ISBN 3-540-55131-X Springer-Verlag Berlin Heidelberg New York Tokyo
ISBN 0-387-55131-X Springer-Verlag New York Heidelberg Berlin Tokyo

© Springer-Verlag Berlin · Heidelberg 1992
Printed in Germany

2142/7130-543210 - Printed on acid-free paper

# Incorporating the Contents into a General Framework

The books on business informatics published by the author in recent years follow a basic logic, which is illustrated in Fig. 01.

Business informatics constitutes the interface between the business applications and information technology.

Reciprocal relationships exist at this interface. On the one hand, information technology needs to be analysed to determine the extent to which new information processing techniques permit new EDP-oriented business application concepts. The influence in this direction is indicated by the arrow heads on the left of Fig. 01. The width of the oval band linking business applications with information technology indicates the significance for business informatics. Thus, business informatics is not primarily concerned with describing the entire world of information technology, but is only interested in those aspects that lead to changes in business application concepts. To these aspects, however, it needs to devote particular attention.

The arrow heads on the right side of the band indicate the influence that EDP-oriented business applications have on information technology. They show that EDP-oriented business applications make demands for further developments in information technology to improve the effectiveness of tis support.

These two directions of influence were both investigated by the author in his book "Principles of Efficient Information Management" which appeared in fourth German edition in 1990, and in second English edition in 1991.

A further conceptual framework analysing the fundamental effects of information technology on business processes was considered in the book "CIM - Towards the Factory of the Future", which also appeared in fourth German edition in 1990, and in second English edition in 1991.

**Both works thus consider EDP-oriented conceptual frameworks, which can provide the starting point for specific EDP-oriented system solutions within the enterprise.**

The implementation of this kind of conceptual framework using the instruments of information technology is effected via information systems. The information system is thus the concrete intermediary between the conceptual framework of business applications and information technology. Since it relates to both the business applications level and information technology, it is correspondingly complex. In order to reduce this complexity, therefore, the information system is broken down.

With respect to the business application views of the information system, a distinction is drawn between the organization, the functions represented, the data, and the control between these three views. At the same time, the description indicates the differing degrees of proximity to the information technology.

The requirements definition transforms available knowledge, which is usually still relatively unstructured, via an EDP-oriented conceptual framework into more formal descriptions. This process is referred to as modelling; its results are then the organization, function, data, and control models. The correspondence between the business applications world and these models is still relatively high, as is indicated by the width of the double arrow in Fig. 01.

In the next step, the requirements definition is confronted with the demands of the EDP techniques, and thus formalized still further. The mutual dependence between the requirements and the resulting design specification should be as small as possible. This means that the working group responsible for preparing the design specification can simply be handed over the requirements definition, and subsequently only minor reconciliation should be necessary.

In the third phase, the design specification is tailored to concrete technical hardware and software architectures. Here, greater interdependences arise in reconciling the requirements definition and the implementation description, which is again expressed by the width of the double arrow. The implementation description has close links with information technology - the requirements definition with the real business applications.

In the book "Enterprise-Wide Data Modelling - Information Systems in Industry" which appeared in third German edition in 1990, and in English edition in 1989, these views and levels of an information system were applied to an industrial firm. The foreground was occupied by the creation of data models, since this is of particular significance for the development of integrated information systems. The other views (organization, function and control views) were given less intensive treatment.

The business relevance of the layered information system concept diminishes with the proximity to the technical implementation. At the same time, the stability of the concepts also diminishes, since the volatile developments in information technology principally affect the technical implementation of information systems. These ideas determined the weighting of the problems handled in the book "Enterprise-Wide Data Modelling - Information Systems in Industry", which is expressed by the diminishing width of the associated field in Fig. 01.

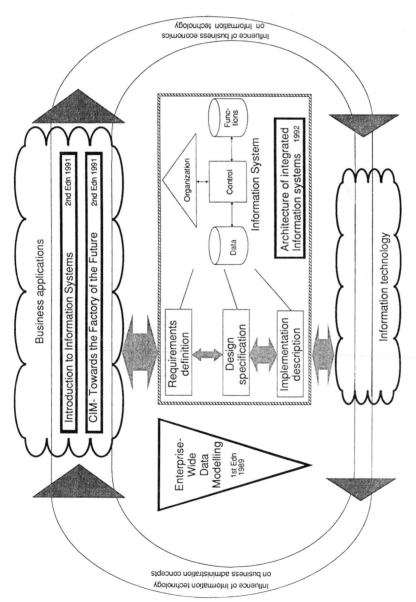

Fig. 01: Categorisation of the author's books within a frame of reference

# Preface

The creation and implementation of integrated information systems involves a variety of collaborators including people from specialist departments, informatics, external advisers and manufacturers. They need clear rules and limits within which they can process their individual sub-tasks, in order to ensure the logical consistency of the entire project. An architecture therefore needs to be established to determine the components that make up the information system and the methods to be used to describe it.

Whereas previously, individual descriptive viewpoints such as the functional representation or the data model have dominated, this book creates an architecture within which the function, organization, and data views of an information system throughout the development phases of the requirements definition, design specification and the implementation description can be given equal treatment.

The ARIS architecture thereby developed is described in concrete terms as an information model within the entity-relationship approach. This information model provides the basis for the systematic and rational application of methods in the development of information systems. Furthermore, it is also the basis for a repository in which the enterprise's application-specific data, organization and function models can be stored.

An essential property of the ARIS architecture is that the various views are not only considered in isolation, but a control view also represents their relationships with each other. As a result, new developments such as distributed databases or object-oriented approaches can be incorporated in the architecture.

I would like to thank Irene Cameron for her careful translation of the German original, and my employees Ralf Heib and Carmen Kächler for their dedicated support in the technical preparation of the manuscript.

Saarbrücken, March 1992                                August-Wilhelm Scheer

# A. Conception of the ARIS Architecture for Integrated Information Systems

The development of application software is considered expensive and both the development time and the planned costs are subject to considerable uncertainty. The tendency therefore exists to remove software development from the sphere of handicrafted one-off production to the organizational form of industrial production which is then logically described as the software factory (see *Balzert, Die Entwicklung von Software-Systemen 1982, p. 5 ff.*).

In this context a multiplicity of methods has been conceived to support the software development process. The methods can be distinguished according to those aspects of the software development process which they aim to support, and according to their chosen perspective on the problem (e.g. data-, event-, or function-oriented). An impression of the number of available methods can be obtained from standard texts on software engineering, e.g. Balzert (see *Balzert, Die Entwicklung von Software-Systemen 1982*), Sommerville *(see Sommerville, Software Engineering 1987)* or from the conference reports of the Working Group 8.1 published by IFIP (see e.g. *Olle/Sol/Tully, Information Systems 1983*).

The multiplicity of methods, which often differ marginally from each other, has led to considerable difficulties in surveying the methods and has tended to impede the development of computerized tools based on these methods. As a result, attempts are being made to create a methodology (theory of methods) for the development methods.

Typical questions which the framework provided by such a methodology should help to answer are (see *Sol, Information Systems Design Methodologies 1983, p. 4; Olle/Hagelstein/MacDonald, Information Systems 1988, p. 2; Brodie/Ridjanovic/Silva, Framework for Information Systems 1983, p. 232)*:

1. Are there really so many fundamentally different ways of designing a computerized information system?
2. If not, how similar are these ways, and if so, why are the ways so different?
3. Is there an optimal way to develop an information system?
4. Where does the development process begin and end?
5. What does the end product of the design process look like?
6. How many levels are needed to achieve a development result?
7. Should only **one** methodology be employed for a specific type of information system or are several methods required for different systems? If so, which criteria should be used to determine the method to be used?

In addition to answering these questions, with the aim of categorising and evaluating the methods, there is another set of reasons for considering ISDMs (Information System Design Methodologies). These reasons result from the fact that in general complex development projects involve several partners who may implement diverse development methods and whose working results overlap. In this situation, only a conceptual framework which allows the categorisation of the various methods, and consequently their conformities and discrepancies, can generate mutual understanding. The fact that such a conceptual framework can, and even must, also lead to uniformity in the use of methods is, of course, also relevant.

Computerized information systems for business application are particularly characterized by an increasingly high degree of complexity. Integrated data processing, which supports the common use of data by diverse applications, and the implementation of comprehensive EDP-oriented global enterprise models (CIM in industrial firms, computerized retail information and control systems in trading firms, electronic banking in banking firms) mean that many internal and external partners are involved in the development of an information system. A conceptual framework, or architecture, is required to allow the coordinated division of labour in the implementation of such projects.

Architecture is generally understood as the art of construction. Applying this concept to information systems implies that the individual building blocks which constitute the information system need to be described in terms of their:
- type,
- functional properties and
- interactions.

The application of the term architecture to information processing concepts is commonplace. Attempts to justify the application of architectural concepts to information systems in etymological terms are made by Krcmar (see *Krcmar, Informationssystem-Architekturen 1990, p. 396*) and Strunz (see *Strunz, Information- und Kommunikationssysteme 1990, p. 441*). However, the author believes that the application of the concept should be regarded as the result of a colloquial understanding rather than in terms of an etymological explanation. Here, associated with the term architecture are concepts such as planning, the following of rules, the organization or coordination of several partners, which correspond to problems within information systems. Furthermore, the term has largely been adopted from the American literature, and is also applied to the description of hardware and database systems (see *Lockemann/Dittrich, Architektur von Datenbanksystemen 1987, p. 87*).

In addition to that part of the architecture which defines the components and their interaction - the "what" that is established in the description of an information system - the "how" must be also established, that is, the procedural method for creating an information system.

An information system architecture facilitates the use of tools for automating the development process. It is common knowledge that the development of large software systems is associated with considerable costs and risks. Consequently, efforts are being made to automate software production by developing a comprehensive set of tools (see e.g. *Olle/Verrijn-Stuart/Bhabuta, Information Systems Life Cycle 1988; Preßmar/Eggers/Reinken, Interaktive Entwurfsmethode 1989, p. 237; Barker, CASE* Method 1990; Hildebrand, Software Tools 1990*).

Many of the methods that are commonly used at present for developing information systems are the result of empirical findings rather than theoretical models. Some of the approaches to developing a methodology also attempt to integrate the existing methods into a conceptual framework, rather than deriving the methodology theoretically.

For this reason, the following treatment derives the architecture of integrated business information systems from a general business application process chain model. The emphasis on the business applications background does not represent a significant restriction. Rather, it emphasizes the considerable significance of the integration idea of information systems, which is typical of business applications, refers to the area from which the vast majority of application examples in this book are taken, and indicates that special applications systems (e.g. process automation) will receive less attention. The **Ar**chitecture of Integrated Information **S**ystems (ARIS) which is developed should therefore be regarded as a generally applicable proposal.

The ARIS architecture constitutes a framework in which integrated applications systems can be developed, optimized and converted into EDP-technical implementations. At the same time, it demonstrates how business administration can examine and analyze information systems in order to translate their contents into EDP-suitable form.

## A.I The Process Chain Model as Starting Point for Developing the Architecture

Process chains provide essential support for business information systems (see *Scheer, Principles of Efficient Information Management 1991, pp. 35*). Examples of process chains are the entire order handling process from order acceptance through material management, production to dispatch, or the development of a product from the initial idea through to the release of the fully tested product for production. The elements of a process chain are the individual processes. A process is an occurrence of some duration which is started by an event and completed by an event. Start and result events thus define the beginning and end of the process (see Fig. A.I.01).

The object of the processing can be the transformation of materials used into products (materials produced). In terms of Gutenberg's theory of production (see *Gutenberg, Die Produktion 1983*), further factors of production - the use of human labour and equipment in the form of production machines or information technology devices - are needed to achieve this transformation. The rules for combining the basic factors are specified as processing rules for describing the process.

Parallel to the process of material transformation, and closely linked with it, is the process of information transformation. The event as an occurrence at a specific point of time (e.g. in the form of a production order) initiates the process of production. In contrast to a process, an event requires neither time nor resources. The result is then the completion of the order as result event and the produced part S5. A result event can also be a change in status of an already familiar object. The order completion report is therefore the change in status of the production order. It is quite possible that several events in conjunction initiate a process, or that several events are the result of a process.

To control the process, conditions in the task environment need to be included, which provide parameters for the processing rules, for example. In the case of production these might be descriptions of the product to be created or the components needed (inventories). During processing these data can be altered, for example, inventories can be reduced by assigning components to the customer order.

Alterations to the conditions in an environment resulting from the processing function are always the consequence of the events generated by the execution of the process. Examples might be the establishment of a new entity (customer, article, etc.) or alterations to an attribute value. This state of affairs characterizes the conventional definition of a process as the transformation of input data into output data. The individual events and the alterations which are based on them only become visible when the processes are described in detail. The alteration represented in Fig. A.I.01 by counter-arrows is thus a rough representation of the transformation process. Only two specific events are highlighted, which represent the start and the result of a process.

Depending on the kind of process, the transformation of either material or information can be predominant. In considering production processes, such as are analysed in the

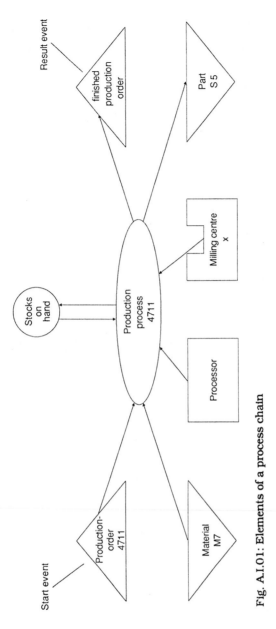

Fig. A.I.01: Elements of a process chain

context of production theory, the material transformation is dominant. In contrast, for more administrative processes, such as order processing, accounting, planning and design, the information transformation process is dominant. It must be emphasized, however, that the two processes are intertwined, that is, material transformation also involves information transformation and alterations to information can also give rise to material alterations. These interdependences are particularly obvious in the case of modern technical production processes, in which machines are controlled by control programs (NC programs) and feedback concerning the execution of the process is automatically recorded by the information system. For this reason, production-oriented and information-oriented equipment are regarded as of equal significance.

Information systems are used to support specific applications. These can be viewed at various levels of abstraction. Typical concepts at the individual levels are shown on the right side of Fig. A.I.02. At level 1 in Fig. A.I.02 the individual instances of the "order handling" process chain are represented. The lowest chain relates to the specific order with the number 4711, the chain only partially presented above it relates to the specific order 4712. The event "receipt of customer order 4711" initiates the processing function "order acceptance" for order 4711. A specific employee from the order processing department who deals with customers is responsible for this. Details of the customer concerned and the article referred to in the order are required for processing.

The result event of order acceptance is an "order confirmation" for order 4711. This then initiates the "order monitoring process" through to dispatch. Details of the relevant article 95 can also be required for order monitoring. At the same time, the order confirmation initiates the production of the article demanded by the customer. This requires the use of material M7 as well as labour and capital.

Abstracting from the individual properties of particular order processes generates the standard process of order handling shown at level 2. Here, the description of the individual processes "order acceptance, order monitoring and production" defines the general rules for the transformation of material and information which are controlled by the specific status of the customer and article data in the way in which they are used. The combination of similar objects into a single concept type is referred to as classification. Similarity between elements arises when elements of the same class can be described by the same characteristics.

The specific individual orders are thus amalgamated into the class ORDER, the individual order acceptances to the class ORDER ACCEPTANCE, etc.

Business information systems are generally described at this second level. Consequently, they relate to specific applications areas and constitute a general processing framework for individual processes.

Further abstraction from the application, i.e. from whether an order processing or an accounting process is being described, generates the general process chain model of level

3. Reference to the application is thereby abandoned and a level reached at which the fundamental structure of the processing of a process chain is described.

The temporally-specific factors, such as order placement or order confirmation are amalgamated into the class EVENT, all time-taking occurrences are amalgamated into the class PROCESS, all environmental descriptions to the class ENVIRONMENTAL CONDITIONS, all materials (auxiliary materials, equipment and other materials) to the class MATERIALS, etc.

The graphic for level 3 does not show all conceivable relationships between the components. Thus, specific employees can be assigned both to organizational units and to equipment, or an event can be explained by relationships between environmental conditions. For example, the event "order placement" can be defined as the relationship between a specific customer as an element of the environment or time. However, the representation provides a clear basis for further analysis.

Since this level contains information about the actual descriptive level of the business information system, it is referred to as the meta-level. At this level approaches, procedures and concepts to be used to describe the underlying application levels are established. At level 2 diverse description procedures can be applied. At level 3, however, the elements to be described by this procedure are fixed.

This abstraction is also a classification, since once again similar objects are amalgamated into conceptual types. The level 2 objects are thereby elements (instances) of the level 3 classes.

The amalgamation into classes is an intellectual procedure and as such not free from subjective elements. For example, intermediate classes could have been formed, in that first the classes "rush orders and normal orders" be established for specific customer orders which would then be amalgamated as the class "orders". This implies that, particularly at level 2, several class hierarchies are possible. The relationships between the individual levels resulting from the classification operation are shown in Fig. A.I.03.

The developed class structure at level 3 is also not the only possible one. However, it does contain the essential concepts for describing the business application and informational facts, and thereby constitutes a suitable starting point for further analysis.

In the following, this initial model will be used to derive an architecture, within which information systems can be described which are then used primarily to provide support for process chains.

8

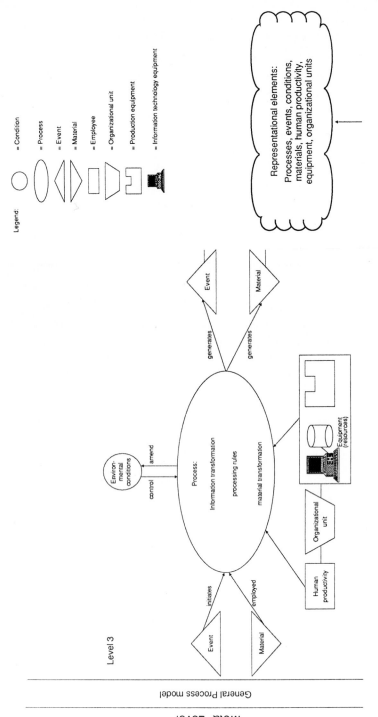

Legend:

○ = Condition

⬭ = Process

◁▷ = Event

▭ = Material

⬠ = Employee

⬡ = Organizational unit

⊐ = Production equipment

▦ = Information technology equipment

Representational elements:
Processes, events, conditions, materials, human productivity, equipment, organizational units

Meta - Level

General Process model

Level 3

Event — generates

Material — generates

Environ-mental conditions — amend / control

Process:
Information transformation
processing rules
material transformation

Event — initiates

Material — employed

Human productivity

Organizational unit

Equipment (resources)

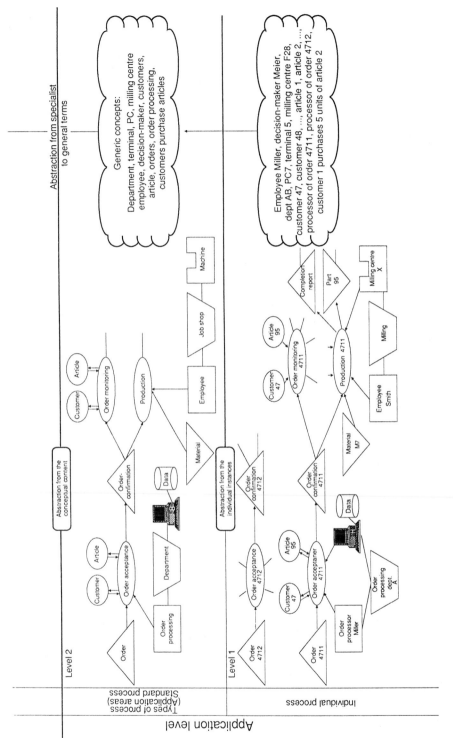

Fig. A.I.02: Levels of abstraction of process chains

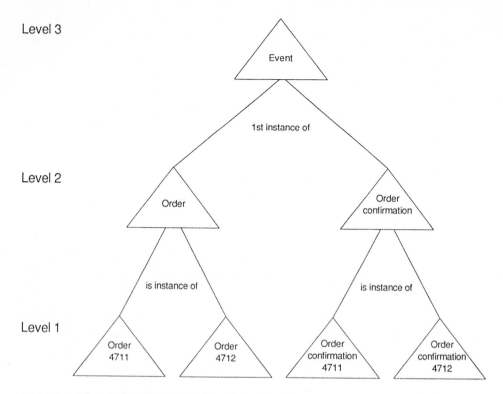

Fig. A.I.03: Relationships between the abstraction levels

Once the ARIS architecture has been established, Part B will consider the individual components in more detail. This will involve more detailed description of level 2, including the descriptive processes commonly used. These will be analyzed and the general elements including their relationships to level 3 will be established. The ARIS architecture provides the framework for this analysis, and must therefore be constructed in such a way that these detailed considerations are also possible.

To this end, the initial model will be further structured, in order to simplify the descriptive subject matter. Thereafter, a descriptive language will be established for describing at level 3 all the objects used at level 2. This also allows all the various software design methods used at level 2, and the constructs that they employ, to be represented in a uniform language.

The architecture provides the framework for storing models of level 2. These are then filed in a meta-database, or a repository.

Level 3, therefore, consists of:

- the general procedural method for deriving the architecture,
- the descriptive building blocks and components (architecture),
- the descriptive language for a detailed description of the building blocks and components for classifying the conceptual world of level 2,
- models for representing the elements of a descriptive approach (meta-models),
- a database for storing the level 2 models described in accordance with the architecture (repository).


## A.II Derivation of the ARIS Architecture by Structuring the Process Chain Model

The components of an information system to be described from the business application standpoint, including their relationships to each other, are therefore conditions, events, and processes; the factors of production: materials, human labour (employees), and equipment (differentiated between production equipment and information technology equipment); and the organizational units to which they are allocated. Since each element can be related to every other element, this generates a complex structure. Multiple relationships can also exist. For example, the relationship between the process and human labour also depends on the equipment provided in support of the execution of the process. Furthermore, relationships can also arise within the elements, indicating how conditions depend on each other, or how events can be linked together, for example.

In order to reduce the complexity, therefore, three steps are undertaken:

1. the abstraction from factors that are irrelevant to information processing,
2. the amalgamation of elements into more general descriptive views.
3. the reduction of relationships using a phased, or procedural, model.


### A.II.1 Concentration on the Transformation of Information

To achieve a reduction of the number of components to be analyzed and to ensure simplicity, the physical material transformation process is no longer treated as an independent descriptive component of the architecture. Instead, it is considered as part of the environment of the process chain, which is described by conditions. The same applies to the production equipment used in the transformation of material. This also enters the informational representation via the concept of the environmental condition.

As a result of the close links between the real and the information transformation, however, information **about** the material transformation process continues to be reflected in the description of the environment conditions. For example, in a PPC system a process chain model for material transformation is represented by bills of materials and routings. Here, the operations to be carried out (e.g. sawing, drilling, milling), the equipment to be used and the materials needed are described. However, these are recorded by a PPC system as environmental descriptions (in the database). The operations in this information transformation process, in which these data are used as environmental conditions, are process planning, routing, production control and factory data collection, for example.

The broad concept "environmental condition" is therefore used to absorb all those components of an information system which are not to be handled from their own descriptive viewpoint.

Human productive capacity - employees - are divided into those involved in the production process, who are also regarded as part of the environment, and those users who are directly involved with the information systems. Fig. A.II.01 indicates this change in perspective by enclosing the elements involved within broken lines. This approach

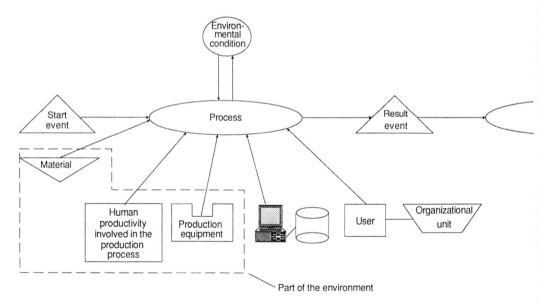

Fig. A.II.01: Elements of the "environmental conditions" component

signifies that, from the information processing viewpoint, the production process is not viewed from the physical standpoint of the use of materials, human labour and equipment, but merely in terms of the data alterations resulting from the physical production process. Thus, only the data-related representation is considered.

The information technology equipment, however, continues to be relevant as the foundation for the information system. The same applies to that human productivity which is directly linked with the information system via the user. The aggregation of employees or equipment into organizational units also continues to be a relevant component.

## A.II.2 Creating Views

The process chain model resulting from the concentration on informationally relevant factors is still complex. Consequently, individual descriptive elements are further combined.

The process-specific view also gives rise to considerable redundancies. The same environmental conditions, events, users, etc., can be responsible for several processes, as was indicated in Fig. A.I.02 for the customer and article descriptions in the case of the detailed order acceptance and order monitoring. In order to avoid these redundancies the process chain model is broken down into individual views, which are then described independently, and thus with less redundancy (see Fig. A.II.02).

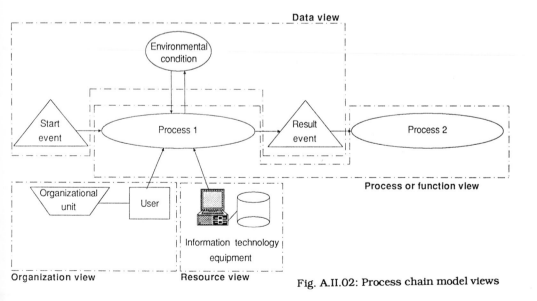

Fig. A.II.02: Process chain model views

First, events and environmental conditions are represented by data. They are represented as information objects using a uniform data view. The recording of events as part of a data view is common to many software development methods (see *Olle/Hagelstein/MacDonald, Information Systems 1988, p. 43*).

The description of process rules and the process structure provides the process or function view. The term "function" is therefore often used interchangeably with the terms "process" or "process chain", because it is often used in the literature in association with functionally-oriented system design. A more precise definition of the terms will be given below (see Section B.II. 1).

Because of their close connections, the two components: user and organizational unit are aggregated into a single element. Users are assigned to organizational units, and these are constructed on the basis of criteria such as "same function" or "same work object". This view is referred to as the organizational view.

Information technology equipment constitutes the fourth descriptive area, the resource view. This reduces the six descriptive elements to four, whereby further simplification is achieved by the concentration of the terms equipment and user on the relationship with information transformation. In creating these views, however, the links between the views are lost. For this reason, an additional view, referred to as "control", will be introduced later to record the relationships between the viewpoints.

In addition to reducing complexity and redundancy within the descriptive subject matter, the formation of views also has the advantage that one component (that is, one view) can already be developed without the other views being available. This means, for example, that later the data model for a system can be created without the functions being comprehensively defined. Insofar as details from one view are absolutely essential for the description of another view these can be established in general form by this view and then further specified by the relevant view.

The division between views cannot always be absolutely strictly maintained, as a result of the relationships existing between them. For example, the description of processes within the function view might also usefully specify events which initiate or result from processes, although these are partially recorded in the data model. The strict requirements of the definition of information objects do not then need to be maintained.

The boundaries between the meta-levels and the description of an application area are not always clear. For example, the organizational viewpoint is on the one hand described as part of the ARIS architecture in the meta-information model, on the other hand "organization" is a business application which can be represented in an application-specific "organization" data model (see *Scheer, Enterprise-Wide Data Modelling 1989, p. 425*)

### A.II.3 Breakdown of the Resource View Using a Phase Model

Given the multiplicity of components, such as CPU, peripherals, networks, programming systems or database systems, the resource view of an information system is particularly broad and multifarious. On the other hand, this view is only of importance from the business application viewpoint in that, as foundation for the information system, it provides framework conditions for the description of the other components and their relationships.

For this reason, the resources are not regarded as an independent descriptive area, but rather, the resource view is handled within each of the other component descriptions. Furthermore, the description of the other views is differentiated according to their proximity to the information technical resources.

This process of transforming the business requirements into the EDP-technical implementation is often described by differentiated phase models (see the 12 stage model in *Olle/Hagelstein/MacDonald, Information Systems 1988, p. 37*, for example). The following treatment adopts a five stage layering approach to implementing and operating a business applications system.

In the first step, an EDP-oriented **semantic starting position** is created. This is the result of an actual analysis of the process chains with planned concepts built upon it. This process chain analysis should make the fundamental benefits of the information system visible. For this reason, at this stage all the views are examined together.

In the second step, a **requirements definition** models the individual viewpoints of the applications system independent of implementation considerations. In the process, descriptive languages are chosen which are sufficiently formalized to provide a starting point for a consistent EDP-technical implementation.

In the third step, the creation of the **design specification**, the requirements definitions are adapted to the demands of the user interfaces of the implementation tools (e.g. database systems, network architectures or programming languages). However, at this point there is still no reference to specific products.

In the course of the fourth step, the **technical implementation description**, the concrete translation of the requirements into physical data structures, hardware components and programming systems is undertaken.

These four phases describe the creation of an information system and are therefore referred to as "build time". Thereafter, the completed system is released for operation, so that the fifth operation and maintenance step can be added, which is referred to as "run time". This run time version of the information system and its tools environment is not further considered below. **This work thus restricts itself to the build time phases of information systems**.

The requirements definition is very closely linked with the business applications sphere, as is shown by the width of the arrow in Fig. A.II.03. It should, however, be created largely independent of the implementation considerations, as is represented by the width of the arrow to the design specification. Both technical implementation and operation and maintenance are, in contrast, closely linked with the "device and product level" of information technology. Changes in information technology have an immediate impact on the kind of implementation and the operation of a system.

The phases cannot always be exactly separated from each other. As a result, the assignment of methods, representations and results of the software design process is not always unambiguous. The phase concept should certainly not be interpreted as a strict sequencing of the development process according to the "waterfall" principle. Rather, a prototyping approach is also explicitly incorporated. But even in the case of evolutionary software development the descriptive levels are given.

Using the phase concept the multifarious relationships between the resource view and the other components can be simplified. Initially, in the first two steps, each component is represented solely from the conceptual viewpoint without implementation restrictions. Thereafter, the factual content is further specified in the framework of the design specification and in the implementation stage it is implemented using specific data processing techniques. Only in the third and fourth phases resource considerations do have an effect. The resources are therefore detailed as required in the course of these descriptions.

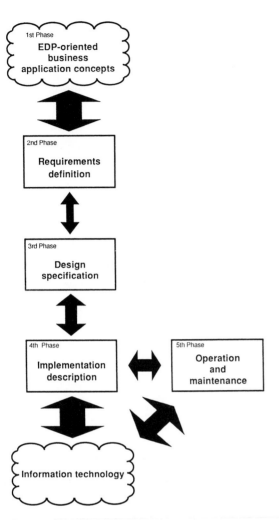

Fig. A.II.03: Description phases dependent on the proximity to information technology

Since in the first step, which consists of the process chain analysis and the creation of the business applications concept, the views are not yet separated, it is not actually part of the ARIS architecture of the information system. The components to be described, therefore, reduce to the model presented in Fig. A.II.04 which consists of the organization, process and data views each with three descriptive levels - the requirements definition, the design specification and the implementation.

By subdividing the procedural model into views, the relationships between these components are lost. However, since elementary relationships exist between data and functions and the organization, these are reintroduced in their own component which intermediates between the elements. This is referred to as the control view.

Since the links between the elements create actions (data, in the form of events, initiate functions, or functions alter data) the term control can serve to indicate this dynamic.

As a result, each component can in the first instance be described independently, the relationships to other components are then handled at the control level. Within control, the three descriptive levels are also established with respect to their proximity to the resources. In this way, the links to the other components can be created at every descriptive level.

Figure A.II.04, therefore, represents the information system architecture. It consists of the following elements: functions, organization, data, and control. All the components are broken down in terms of their proximity to the information technology resources into the descriptive levels: requirements definition, design specification and implementation description.

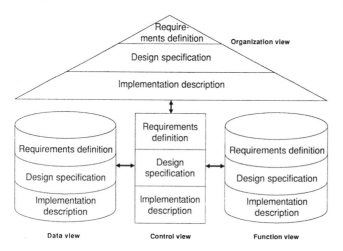

Fig. A.II.04: ARIS architecture

## A.III  Representation of Information Models

Once the building blocks of the ARIS architecture for integrated information systems have been established, it is necessary to determine how their functionality can be described in greater detail.

In order to ensure that the interdependences between the individual blocks can be consistently analysed and modelled, it is necessary to choose a uniform descriptive language which is applied to all of the blocks. It is true that individual representational methods, such as data models, hierarchy diagrams, flow charts, or organization charts, have been developed to describe data, functions, and organizational aspects; however, they relate to the factual representation, that is, level 2 in Fig. A.I.02. At the meta-level, that is, the description of the elements of the information system itself, a uniform language can be applied if it is capable of abstracting from the level-specific contents and reducing the methods to the objects to be represented and the relationships between them. Consequently, a descriptive language is chosen which for each block establishes merely the elements to be described and their relationships to each other.

Chen's Entity-Relationship Model (ERM) (see *Chen, Entity-Relationship Model 1976*) is generally suitable for representing objects and their relationships. Although it was developed for representing data structures for applications systems, it can also be used to describe the meta-level.

Using the uniform descriptive language of the ERM the objects and their relationships within the individual views can be represented. This description is referred to as the information model, or the meta-information model.

Simultaneously, the conceptual description of a database is established, in which the specific applications developed within this architecture can be stored. That is, the organization, function, data and control models of an application area, defined at level 2 of Fig. A.I.02, are held as instances of the database constructed on the basis of the information model. Such a database containing this kind of model is referred to as a **repository**. The term "repository" became popular around 1989 with the announcement of the IBM software development concept AD/CYCLE (see e.g. *Winter/Maag, AD/Cycle 1990; Fosdick, Ten Steps To AD/CYCLE 1990*). The repository contains models developed in the ARIS architecture for the functions, organizations, and data, and their links with the descriptive level 2 in Fig. A.I.02 (that is, the generalized applications level) for the requirements definitions, design specifications and implementation descriptions. The repository therefore constitutes the heart of an information system, and the information model of the repository is correspondingly significant, since its constructs determine the descriptive power for modelling the information system.

The ERM consists of the elements entity or object types (represented by boxes) and relationship types (represented by rhombi). The relationship types are differentiated into the cardinalities 1:n, 1:1, n:m, and m:1. Fig. A.III.01 represents a rough information model of the ARIS architecture using these simple elements. The individual views are described by the object and relationship types representing them. The individual views are each presented within bold frames. As well as the function, data, organization and control views, the resource view is also explicitly represented. This implies that the gradual proximation to the resource level is not yet expressed in terms of a phase concept, but is generated by the relationship types "TRANSFORMATION, EXECUTION" between the entity type RESOURCES and the other views. This short-cut has the advantage that no terms need to be adopted from the design specification or implementation concept. The information model of Fig. A.III.01 gives a preliminary introduction into the means of representation and should be useful in making comparisons with other architectural concepts. Below, it will be refined considerably.

The starting point for the functional model of Fig. A.III.01 are the enterprise goals which are to be pursued within the information system, or within the process chains and problem-solving approaches it represents. The enterprise goals are generally of hierarchical form. Global goals, such as "profit maximization", "winning a given share of the market" or "achieving a certain rate of growth" generate derived sub-goals such as "achieving a given turnover", "reducing costs by a certain amount" or "attaining a given product quality level".

The structure of the interdependent goals forms an n:m relationship within the entity type ENTERPRISE GOALS.

Certain functions must be carried out to achieve these goals. Examples of such functions are order processing, production or controlling. These can in turn be supported by derived sub-functions. The linking of functions with each other, and the supportive nature of functions with respect to goals, generate an n:m relationship within the entity type FUNCTION, as well as an n:m relationship between FUNCTION and ENTERPRISE GOALS.

On the left side the model of the data structures is presented. The entity type INFORMATION OBJECT refers to the object described by attributes within a database. It comprises events and conditions which can be represented by data. Relationships exist between information objects such as ORDERS, CUSTOMERS, etc. (e.g. which customer placed which order). These are expressed by an n:m relationship within the term INFORMATION OBJECT. Information objects which in terms of their contents belong to a self-contained area can be amalgamated into a data model. Since these may overlap, an n:m relationship exists between data model and information object.

The central concept in the model of the organization view is the organizational unit. This can be defined as a department, post, or a larger unit such as an operational area on up to the entire enterprise. The structure of decision making powers or affiliation relationships between these areas gives rise to an n:m relationship within the entity type ORGANIZATIONAL UNIT. The n:m relationship thereby allows an area to be subordinate to several areas. This is the case, for example, if a factory is responsible for several higher level product areas.

The relationships between the three components are taken into account at the control level.

Functions can be interpreted as the transformation of input data into output data. Events initiate functions and are also the result of functions. These three interdependences are represented as relationships between INFORMATION OBJECT and FUNCTION.

The interdependence between ORGANIZATIONAL UNIT and FUNCTION is expressed by the PROCESSING ASSIGNMENT. Organizational units can be assigned to certain views of the INFORMATION OBJECTS, which is expressed by the relationship type DATA VIEW.

The information technology is represented by the entity type IT-RESOURCES. It is not broken down further, since the description of the relationships occupies the foreground. The relationship type TRANSFORMATION, EXECUTION is always assigned to each of the three models, so that their description within the views can be effected within the phase model in accordance with the architecture developed.

To represent these interdependences Chen's simple ERM model is extended, since relationships will be formed between the relationship types at the control level and the entity type RESOURCES. In this process the relationship types are first redefined as entity types and enclosed within boxes.

The meta-information model as ERM thus describes the objects of an information system (entity types) and the relationships existing between them. It describes all the views of the ARIS architecture developed here (functions, organization, data and control) through the development levels (process chain analysis, requirements definition, design specification and implementation).

At the same time, it constitutes the conceptual schema of a database of the repository for storing the relevant models at the applications level (that is, level 2 of Fig. A.I.02).

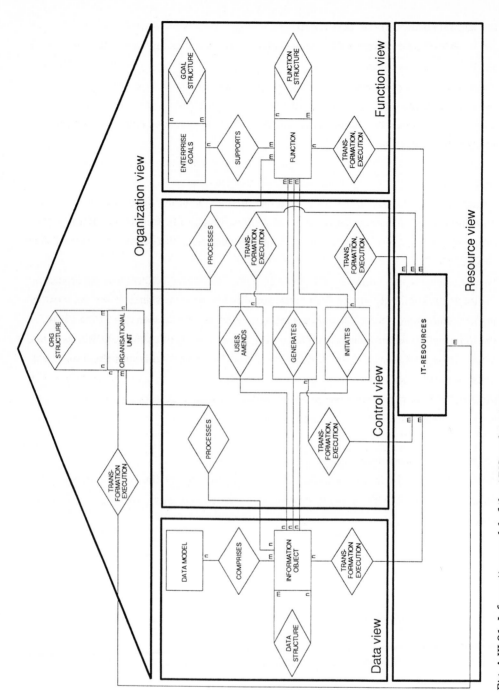

Fig. A.III.01: Information model of the ARIS architecture.

The four components of the meta-level

- general procedural model,
- ARIS architecture,
- descriptive language and ARIS information model,
- repository

are thus developed (see Fig. A.III.02) and can be used as a basis for comparison with other architectural concepts.

First of all, the general procedural model, which contains the basic structure of the process descriptions, establishes the levels to be described (ARIS architecture). For each view, information models containing the objects to be described and their relationships, are created with the help of the ERM descriptive language. Together, these generate the ARIS information model.

The repository is a database whose conceptual schema corresponds to the information models. The data stored contain the descriptions from level 2, that is, e.g. the process and data models for specific applications such as PPC, sales, etc., but not their contents. Whereas the terms CUSTOMER, PART, EQUIPMENT are stored in the repository as entity types of a PPC model, for example, specific instances, that is, the individual customers, parts and equipment entities, are stored in the PPC applications databases.

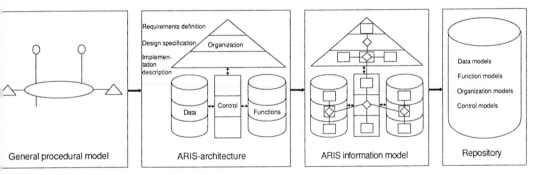

Fig. A.III.02: Components of the meta-level

## A.IV Comparison of ARIS with other Architectural Concepts

Before the associated information models are developed in more detail, the ARIS architecture which has been created will be compared with other architectures.

The approach referred to as the IFIP WG 8.1 architecture has been constructed by a group of experts working for many years on the methodology of information systems, and has been refined into a comprehensive information model. The CIM-OSA architecture is being developed in the context of a large ESPRIT project and is completed up to the description of components. The information model is not yet available.

Some approaches in the literature are either still being developed, are intended only as a rudimentary introduction to a method description, or are merely concerned with special problems. Proposed architectures from computer suppliers are published in association with development tools or development concepts. Up to now these have in general been pragmatic in approach, but some have the character of genuine information models.

The information model of the IBM AD/CYCLE concept is expected to have greater impact as regards factual standardization, but it is thus far only partially available.

Insofar as these approaches have already been described as information models, they will be considered here - at least in excerpt. The models are not considered in detail for reasons of space. Instead, the aim is to give a basic impression of the level of detail. It is striking that all the ERM approaches are based on the Bachmann notation and as a result, their semantic interpretation is restricted as compared with the notation used here.

### A.IV.1 IFIP WG 8.1 Architecture

A comprehensive methodology for developing information systems, described in the form of an information model, is presented by Olle et al. (see *Olle/Hagelstein/MacDonald, Information Systems 1988*). The seven authors of the investigation are members of a task group of IFIP (International Federation for Information Processing), in particular the working group WG 8.1 titled "Design and Evaluation of Information Systems" of the technical committee TC 8 with the title "Information Systems".

The working group WG 8.1 had held several conferences between 1980 and 1987 on questions of the methodology of information systems (see the conference reports *Olle/Sol/Tully, Information Systems 1983; Olle/Verrijn-Stuart/Bhabuta, Information Systems Life Cycle 1988*, for example). The task group consists of both scientists and practitioners who are intensively concerned with information system issues.

In developing the methodology no special development methods for information systems are discussed or classified, rather, a methodology is constructed on the basis of the wide experience of the task group members which aims to incorporate as many approaches as possible. A selection of well-known methods is presented in the appendix, including IDA

(Interactive Design Approach), IEM (Information Engineering Methodology), IML (Inscribed High Level Petri Nets), JSD (Jackson System Development), NIAM (Nijssen's Information Analysis Method) PSL/PSA (Problem Statement Language/Problem Statement Analyser), SADT (Structured Analysis and Design Technique) and Yourdan.

The methodology developed broadly corresponds to the term architecture as it is used here. It is also described with the help of an entity-relationship model (albeit with restricted semantics).

The methodology consists (similarly to ARIS) of two fundamental components: the perspectives and the levels of an information system life-cycle.

The views are differentiated into (see Fig. A.IV.01)
- data-oriented
- process-oriented, and
- behaviour-oriented

perspectives. The creation of these views is based not so much on analytical derivation, but rather aims to take into account the points of emphasis of the well-known methods for developing information systems (see *Olle/Hagelstein/MacDonald, Information Systems 1988, p. 12 f.*).

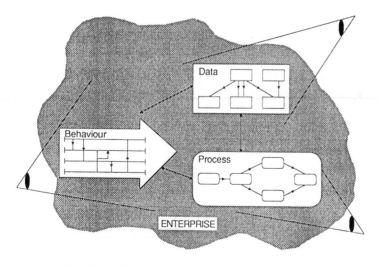

Fig. A.IV.01: IFIP architecture views

from: *Olle/Hagelstein/MacDonald, Information Systems 1988, p. 12*

In the data-oriented view the entity types and their attributes are considered. The process-oriented perspective describes processes (business activities) including their predecessor and successor relationships. In the behaviour-oriented perspective events along with their predecessor and successor relationships are examined.

In addition to the isolated description of the views, interdependences between the views are also investigated.

Alongside the views, the individual stages of the process of developing an information system form the second element of the methodology. From a comprehensive 12 stage life-cycle model (see *Olle/Hagelstein/MacDonald, Information Systems 1988, p. 37*) the following three stages
- information systems planning,
- business analysis,
- system design

have been selected, and the last two examined more closely as the basis of the methodology.

Information systems planning refers to the strategic planning of an information system. In the business analysis context an existing information system for an entire enterprise or some sub-area thereof is analyzed. This process is therefore descriptive rather than prescriptive.

At the system design stage the information system is created. Following this, the EDP implementation is effected at the stage of construction design, but Olle does not consider this further (see *Olle/Hagelstein/MacDonald, Information Systems 1988*).

Comparing this with the ARIS architecture, there are areas of correspondence and divergence. The two-dimensional approach of views and development stages corresponds to that of the ARIS architecture. There are differences within the instances, however. For example, Olle et al. do not explicitly present the organization view, but handle it, albeit in rudimentary form, in the course of the discussion of activities (see *Olle/Hagelstein/MacDonald, Information Systems 1988, p. 58*). The process definition corresponds largely to the function definition undertaken here. Data and functions, or events and functions, are also clearly separated from each other.

The control view introduced here is partially dealt with by linking the three views. For example, the combination of events and processes covers the problems referred to below as event control (see *Olle/Hagelstein/MacDonald Information Systems 1988, p. 95*, and Section B.II.4.1.2.1 below).

The business analysis stage corresponds in part to the first phase of the ARIS "process chain analysis", but goes further, in that it presupposes a more intensive actual analysis in the course of which similar graphical descriptive methods are already employed as are used in the development of the planned design.

The system design stage is a mixture of the requirements definition and design specification phases of ARIS, whereby the emphasis tends to be placed on the design specification. The neglect of the requirements definition can be explained by the fact that the business analysis is carried out so thoroughly. It is true that it is principally handled descriptively (actual analysis), however, the concepts and interdependences developed can be carried over to the planned concept. For this reason, the "business analysis" can be regarded as equivalent to large parts of the requirements definition.

In developing the ERMs for representing the methodology, particular emphasis is placed on the differentiation between the names and the actual descriptive objects entity type, attribute, activity, etc. Sets such as entity type names, attribute names and activity names are assigned to the descriptive objects via relationships. As a consequence, multi-lingual versions can be handled, for example, as well as synonyms and homonyms. An impression of the representational form and the degree of detail of the methodology is given in Fig. A.IV.02, which represents the data perspective of the business analysis stage as an ERM.

An additional distinction is that of whether the defined objects are to be filled with elements by the system developer in the course of a system design, or whether predetermined instances are already established within the methodology. These are shown in the representation within bold frames. For example, instances of the term "entity type" in the data model context are established for an applications area by the system developer by terms such as customer, article, supplier, etc. In contrast, the instances ONLINE or BATCH are already predetermined for the entity type "processing form" by the methodology, and are not introduced by the system developer. In this case, the system developer simply carries out assignments of the processing form to the transactions he has created. In Fig. A.IV 02 this applies to entity types such as "relationship class", whose permitted cardinalities are determined in advance.
Relationship types are represented by so-called "cross entity types" and indicated by double sidelines.

28

The essential differences between the IFIP model and the ARIS architecture are:

- the absence of the organization view,
- the absence of the implementation phase,
- the absence of a systematically handled control view.

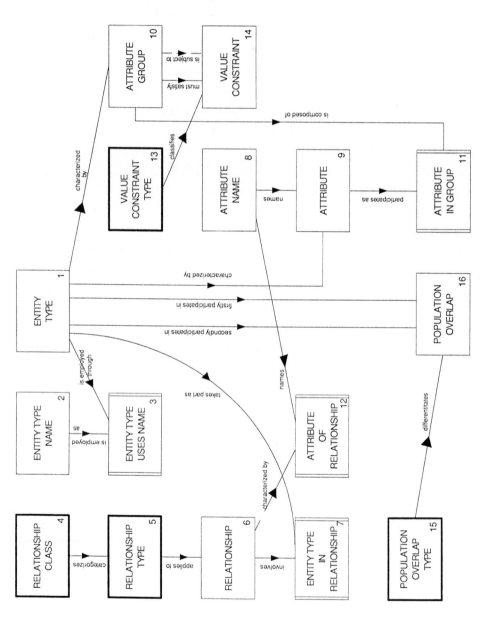

Fig. A.IV.02: Information model of the business analysis data view

from: Olle/Hagelstein/MacDonald, Information Systems 1988, p. 61

**A.IV.2  CIM-OSA Architecture**

The architecture of information systems is the subject of intensive consideration by the CIM-OSA (Open System Architecture for CIM) research project supported by the EEC (see *ESPRIT Consortium AMICE (eds.), Open System Architecture 1989*). Fig. A.IV.03 represents the framework model that has been developed. CIM-OSA differentiates between three dimensions, which are described by the three axes of a cube. The vertical direction (stepwise derivation) describes three descriptive levels of a phase concept (requirements definition, design specification, implementation description).

These levels correspond to the concepts within the ARIS architecture, although not in terms of their contents. For instance, optimization of the user requirements is undertaken at the design specification level of CIM-OSA. In the ARIS approach this has already been undertaken in the context of the requirements definition, so that the result of the requirements definition can be implemented in unmodified form. At the level of the design specification optimization is undertaken simply to exploit the data processing performance criteria.

In the context of the horizontal dimension, "stepwise instantiation", a gradual individualization of the concepts is examined. First, fundamental requirements (generic requirements) are defined which, in the following step, are then specified as concrete branch-specific requirements (partial requirements), such that they can be broken down in the third step into individual enterprise specifics (particular requirements). This perspective indicates that in the CIM-OSA context general elements are first defined as standards, which are then amalgamated into branch-specific reference models and finally used to develop enterprise-specific solutions.

Within the ARIS architecture the question of the level of detail at which an information system should be developed is initially of no consequence, since a general information model is to be developed. In particular, no application-specific reference models are included which are established as instances in the framework model developed and stored in the repository. This also indicates, therefore, that the CIM-OSA architecture is a mixture of general methodological information system questions and application-specific CIM issues.

The third dimension, "stepwise generation", describes the various views of an information system. This approach is similar in its aims to that of the ARIS approach, but not necessarily in all its results. CIM-OSA breaks down the descriptive views into the

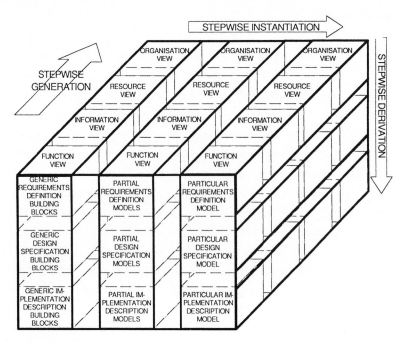

Fig. A.IV.03: CIM-OSA Framework

from: *ESPRIT Consortium AMICE (eds.), Open System Architecture 1989, p. 46*

"function view", "information view", "resource view" and "organization view". The function view refers to the description of processes, and the information view to the data perspective. The resource view describes both the information technical and the production technical resources, and the organization view the organizational aspects.

CIM-OSA, therefore, also undertakes a breakdown of the entire complex into various views. However, the level putting these views back together, such as the control component proposed in ARIS, is missing. As a result, in CIM-OSA the descriptions of the individual views are not always mutually exclusive. For example, the description of resources also handles the allocation of resources to functions (see *ESPRIT Consortium AMICE (eds.), Open System Architecture 1989, p. 75*) and resources are also described in the context of the organization view (see *ESPRIT Consortium AMICE (eds.), Open System Architecture 1989, p. 91*).

In spite of these objections, the CIM-OSA concept of developing an architecture for describing information systems, which allows the systematic incorporation of contents in the form of standardized reference models through to software generation, must meet with approval.

The meta-models for the function and data views are shown in Fig. A.IV.04 and A.IV.05.

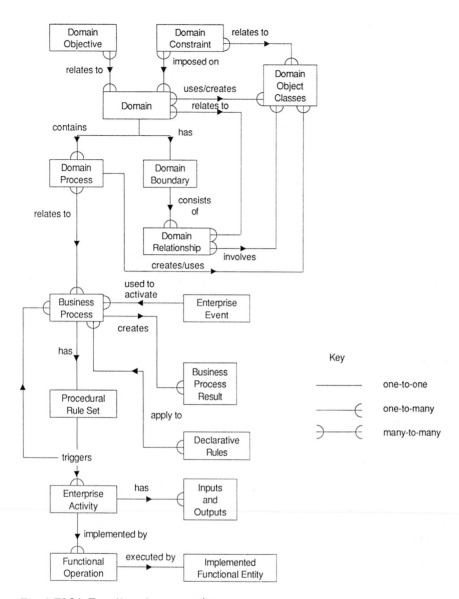

Fig. A.IV.04: Function view concepts

     from: *Jorysz/Vernadat, CIM-OSA Part 1: total enterprise modelling and function view 1990, p. 151*

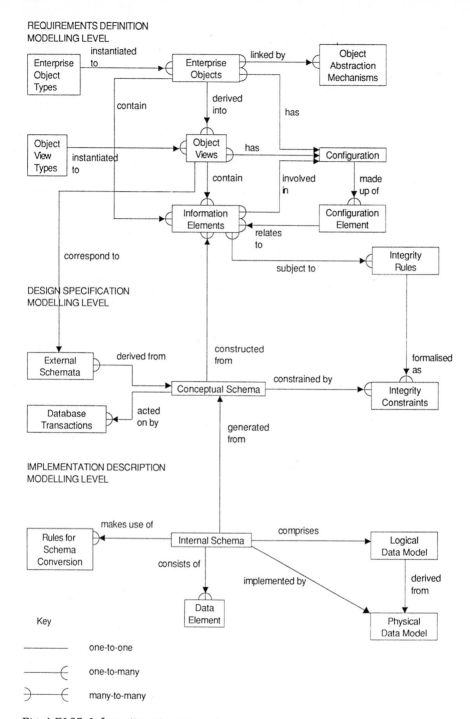

REQUIREMENTS DEFINITION
MODELLING LEVEL

DESIGN SPECIFICATION
MODELLING LEVEL

IMPLEMENTATION DESCRIPTION
MODELLING LEVEL

Fig. A.IV.05: Information view concepts

from: *Jorysz/Venadat, CIM-OSA Part 2: information view 1990, p. 159*

## A.IV.3 Further Architectural Approaches in the Literature

In the context of the CC RIM research program, a working group of practitioners and scientists at the Hochschule St. Gallen has developed a meta-model as a reference model for comparing diverse software development methods (see *Gutzwiller/Österle, Referenz-Meta-Modell Analyse 1990; Gutzwiller/Österle, Referenzbeispiel Analyse 1990*).

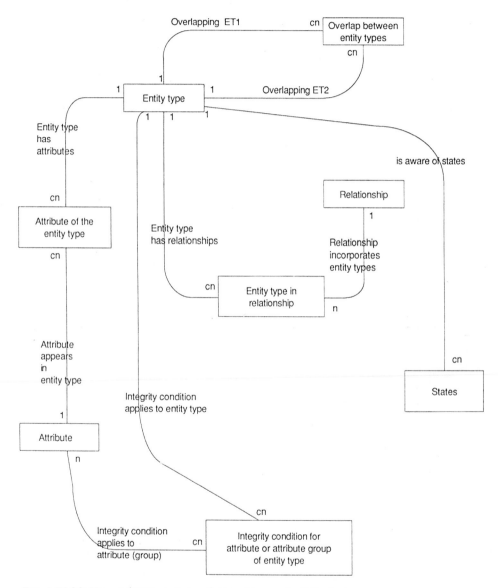

Fig. A.IV.06: View 4 (entity types, relationships and attributes)

from: *Gutzwiller/Österle, Referenz-Meta-Modell Analyse 1990, p. 9*

The model consists of five views, whereby the first three constitute a functional, the fourth a data-oriented, and the fifth a behaviour-oriented perspective.

The approach comprises 36 entity types and 61 relationship types in an ERM. To demonstrate the level of detail the ERM for view 4 (data view) is presented in Fig. A.IV.06. The model is particularly based on Olle's results (see *Olle/Hagelstein/MacDonald, Information Systems 1988*), the entity types used are developed with great detail and precision, and a comprehensive information model can be expected on conclusion of the project.

In addition to efforts aimed explicitly at the development of a meta-information model, work on software development methods can also provide explicitly stated or implicitly contained architectural references. It would be excessive to discuss these in detail, however, since the aim of developing an information model is precisely to facilitate the categorization of this multiplicity of methods. Many of the methods only consider the function and data views (see Fig. A.IV.07, for example), others place greater emphasis on the event view (see *McMenamin/Palmer, Strukturierte Systemanalyse 1988*, for example).

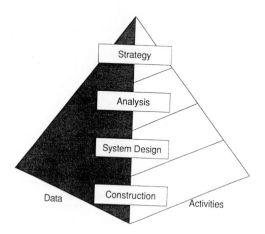

Fig. A.IV.07: The information systems pyramid
from: *Martin, Information Engineering, Planning and Analysis 1990, p. 2*

The KADS (Knowledge Acquisition and Documentation Structuring) approach (see *Breuker/Wielinga/van Someren, Model Driven Knowledge Acquisition 1987*) was developed within the ESPRIT project P 1098 on the generation of knowledge based systems. At the start the emphasis lay in the area of knowledge acquisition and structured documentation. In the course of the project, however, it was extended to the areas of knowledge modelling, including requirements analysis, and system design.

In terms of the analysis of information systems architectures, the first phase of the KADS approach, and within this the creation of the conceptual model, is of greatest interest. The project is not yet completed, but this phase is furthest developed (for a more detailed description see *Aue/Baresch/Keller, URMEL 1990*).

Architectures for the data view are particularly pronounced. These provide a basis for the design of database systems. Typical proposals are layer models, such as that in the ANSI/SPARC proposal. It consists of three levels (see Fig. A.IV.08). At the intermediate conceptual level the logical data structures are represented in a common schema. The individual portions of this model held by the user (human user or program) are defined in external schemata. The internal level contains the implementable representation of the data.

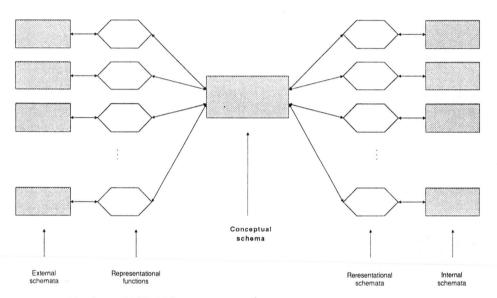

Fig. A.IV.08: The ANSI/SPARC norm proposal

from: *Jablonsky, Datenverwaltung in verteilten Systemen 1990, p. 66*

The architecture pursues the aim of ensuring the highest possible level of data independence. This is understood to mean that the user is protected from detrimental effects of changes in the system environment. These only affect the internal level (implementation level) and do not influence the conceptual level.

Since the ANSI/SPARC rough architecture is intended for developing database systems, the conceptual level, that is, the application-oriented design of the data structures is not included. Accordingly, it is superimposed on the data processing model level. As a result, the conceptual level is largely identical with the level 2 of the data view in the ARIS architecture. The external user view, in contrast, needs to be interpreted as the link between the user as organizational unit or as program (module), and localized in the data processing model of the control view. The internal implementation level corresponds once more to the implementation level of the data view.

### A.IV.4 Architecture Proposals from Computer Suppliers

The information system architecture developed by IBM in the course of their AD/CYCLE concept consists, insofar as this is currently clear, of four components:
- process structure,
- data flow,
- data structure,
- data type (see *Hazzah, Application Development 1990*).

A process describes a business activity and can be broken down into sub-processes. Important characteristics of the process are terms such as external agent, information store, information port, and junction. An external agent is a process which is not a component of the model under consideration, but with which relationships exist. An information store is a logical database in which a process can either store or access information. A junction is a special process which can either break down or amalgamate information. An information port is a link from a process to the outside world, which may also be another process. This allows information flows to be channelled through several processes. An initial impression of the awaited information model is given in the section referred to in the literature quoted. Which data a special process may or may not access is established in the context of the data flow components. Thus, "views" of the data are constructed.

In the data structure context, entity types and their relationships are defined. On the basis of the collaboration with Bachman, a Bachman version of the entity relationship approach is supported. This implies, for example, that relationships are not allowed to carry descriptive attributes. The reason given for this "slimmed-down" application of modelling constructs is that it achieves easier interpersonal independence of the modelling.

Nevertheless, the basic architecture of the information model permits the use of richer constructs, even in the sense of the extended entity relationship model. For example, complex objects can be defined as a combination of entity types, and relationship types that have been introduced can be reinterpreted as entity types. As a result of the collaboration with diverse IBM partners, a diversity of semantic approaches is to be expected.

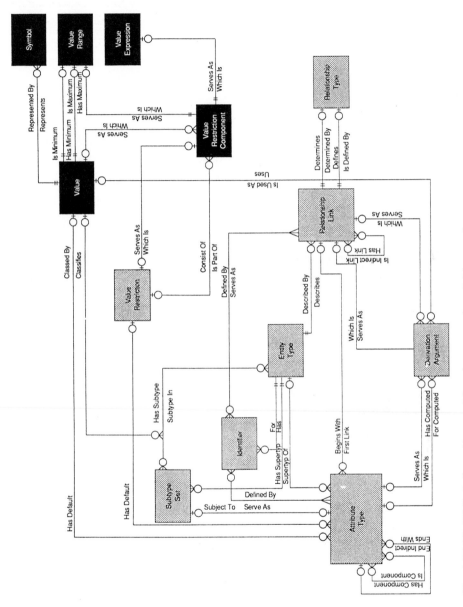

Fig. A.IV.09: IBM's Information model: enterprise submodel (excerpt)

from: *Hazzah, Application development 1990*

38

In the data type context the data elements and their domains and integrity conditions are established.

It is noticeable that the term function is not used in this architecture. Instead, the term process is widely used. Relationships between data and processes are defined within the process model and the data flow model. By defining the data flow approach **alongside** the process and data structure definitions a "control level" between these two components is introduced.

An explicit incorporation of an organization model is not undertaken. Fig. A.IV.09 shows an excerpt from the data view of IBM's information model published by Hazzah.

The IBM architecture is a multi-level structure (see Fig. A.IV.10). Constructs are defined in the repository manager context and constitute the basic system, which quasi serves as a language for modelling the higher levels. The constructs thus provided allow IBM's partners to create reference models for the four views mentioned in the next layer of the modelling level. At the next level up, the third level, the user can then develop his own applications model from the reference model. Thus, there are similarities with the "stepwise instantiation" view of the CIM-OSA architecture.

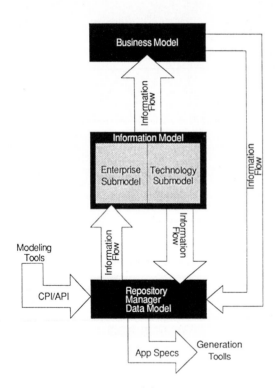

Fig. A.IV.10: 3-level model

from: *Hazzah, Application development 1990, p. 93*

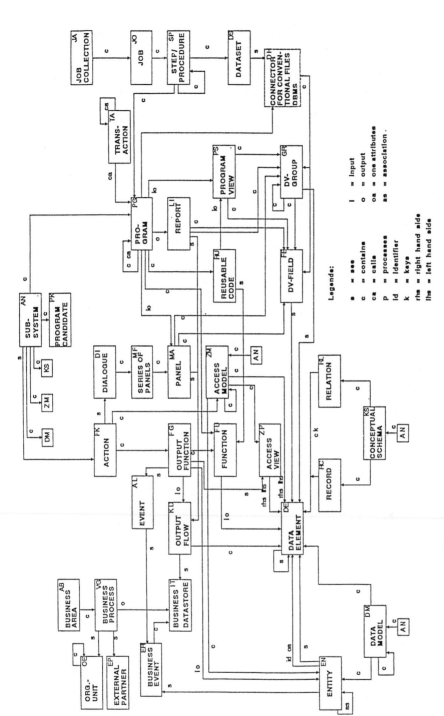

Fig. A.IV.11: ERM information model of the supplier msp

Source: *msp*

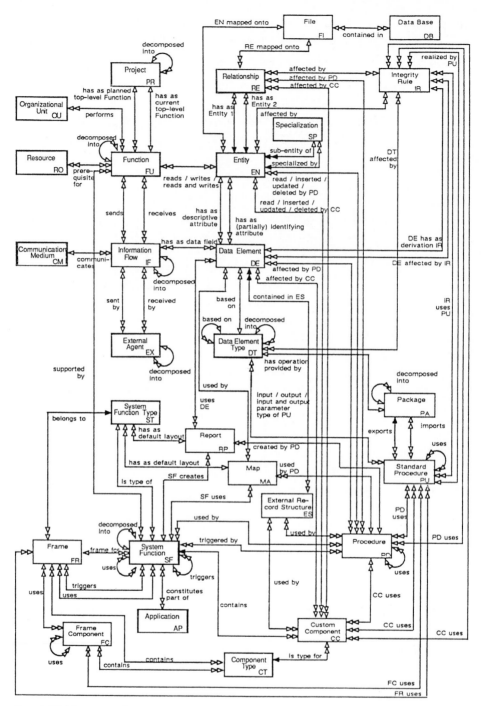

Fig. A.IV.12: ERM information model from Software AG

Source: *Software AG*

The repository manager administers the user's information models. At the same time, CPI (Common Programming Interface) and API (Application Programming Interface) are available as tools for providing run-time interpretation of data stored in the repository.

Completely formulated information models have also been published by the suppliers of software development tools. Figs. A.IV.11 and A.IV.12 present ERM information models from the suppliers msp (Management Software Products) and Software AG. They deal with many of the problems addressed by ARIS, but not within a clearly structured architecture.

The DOMINO procedural method (see *Siemens (eds.), GRAPES-SD (SINIX) 1989*) adopts a graphically oriented approach. The method support accompanies the entire software development process. Essential architectural system components are:

- structure,
- process,
- information, and
- interface with the outside world.

Structure refers to the static composition of a system, including its communication relationships.
A process describes the behaviour of the system.
The term information refers to the data structure.
The representation of these components is supported by seven diagram and table types, which are created using the object-oriented graphical language GRAPES 86. The consistency of the complete description of a model can then be checked automatically using simulation studies. This concept also attempts to incorporate object-oriented approaches, but it is generally neutral as regards methods, i.e., it is capable of supporting various design processes such as SA, SADT, and the developments therefrom.

In comparison with the architecture developed here, there are correspondences in the definition of the life-cycle model. An explicit consideration of the organizational components is missing, however. The relationships between data and functions are represented in the process components.

In comparison with the other architectures presented, the ARIS architecture appears to allow a clear and simple categorization of the factors to be described. In addition, the introduction of the control component allows the links between the isolated component descriptions to be generated, and ensures the consistent and complete description of an information system.

## A.V Incorporating the Procedural Model for Creating Information Systems

The ARIS architecture that has been developed determines how applications systems can be described. Examples of applications systems are systems for production planning and control (PPC), sales management, accounting, etc. But the creation of an information system is in itself an application which can be represented within the architecture. The processes for creating an information system are thus the result of the views and phases that have been developed. Fig A.V.01 presents the corresponding procedural model, consisting of processes and events. The structuring relationships are established such that the function, organization and data views of one phase can be designed out in parallel, but the control view presupposes completion of the others. Other orderings are also conceivable, which in the case of a detailed breakdown of processes into substeps could take a more refined, overlapping form. Within processes, for example, various levels of detail can be differentiated within the development. The impression of a fixed phase concept such as the waterfall model should not be created, but rather the recognition that other development forms, such as prototyping, are also possible by using the appropriate structuring relationships.

In addition to processes and events, environmental conditions, organizational units and resources can also be incorporated in the model.

Fig. A.V.02 presents a detailed excerpt for the individual project of creating of an information system for production planning and control, analogous to Fig. A.I.02 at level 1 and 2. Here, it is assumed that the creation of the data model must precede the creation of the function model.

The start event for the procedure is a project order for creating a new PPC system. The human contribution is expressed by the specialist staff and system analysts involved.

The equipment is represented by the data processing systems for function and data modelling used by the developers. The modelling is based on the structures placed in the repository.

In the course of subsequent design specification activities, tools for supporting the normalization of data structures or for modularizing function description can be used. In the course of implementation programming languages, program generators and database systems are employed.

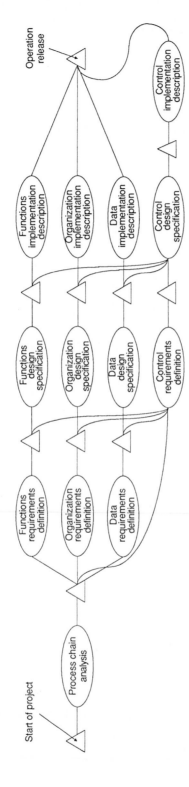

Fig. A.V.01: Procedural model of the ARIS architecture

At level 2 the representation is freed from the specific instances of the PPC system, and the standard process of the procedural model is specified for the segment under consideration.

At the next level of abstraction the general process model of level 3 is generated, which has already been presented in Fig. A.I.02, as the starting point for the development of the ARIS architecture. Thus, this architecture also applies to the procedural model for creating information systems.

The **data view** is constructed from the milestones of the procedural model, that is, from the events which always initiate or complete a process, and from the description of the environmental conditions, that is, the working results in the form of models of the applications system.

The **process view** is derived from the building blocks of the information system architecture.

The **organization view** establishes the departments and employees involved in each process.

The **resource view** relates to the tools to be used in creating an information system.

Fig. A.V.03 indicates the views developed within the architecture for the process "development of the function model requirements definition" selected from the standard procedure.

The data view of the process model consists of the start and end events as well as the existing and newly created function descriptions.

This applies analogously to the other processes. The data views thereby record the working results and thus establish the objects to be described and their relationships.

The data views of the procedural model are, therefore, largely identical with the (meta-) information model of level 3 in Fig. A.I.02. At the same time, they constitute the database schema for the design tools to be used in creating the application model. Thus, the information technology tools play a double role. On the one hand programming languages or database systems support the information systems, and on the other hand they serve as design tools in the creation of the individual descriptions within the procedural model for information systems.

Since the components of the ARIS architecture are now processes within the procedural model, each component can itself be described in the components of the architecture, as shown in Fig. A.V.03. This is further elucidated in Fig.V.04 for the creation of a PPC system. A data model for creation of the requirements definition for the data views of the

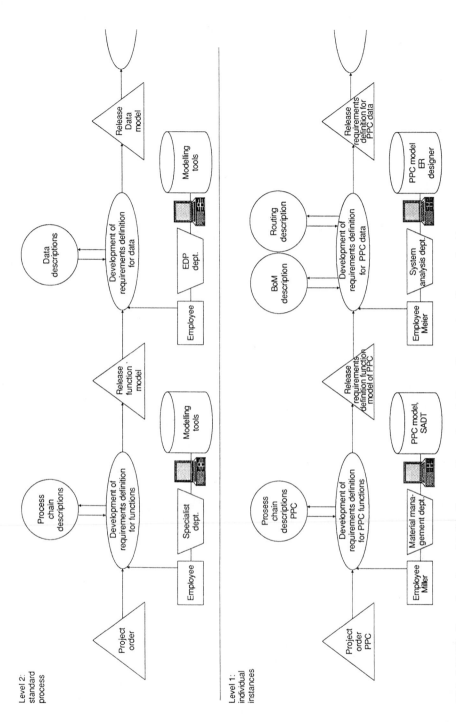

Level 2:
standard
process

Level 1:
individual
instances

Fig. A.V.02: Procedural model for the creation of an information system for production
planning and control

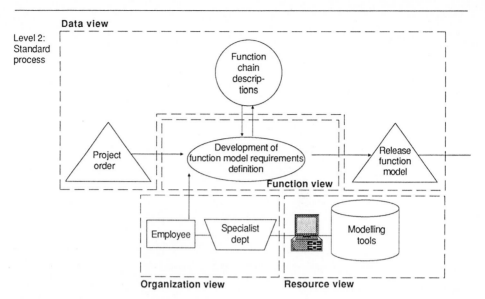

Fig. A.V.03: Procedural model views

PPC system is created with the help of the ERM. From the perspective of the procedural model this process "create requirements definition data view" is itself described in all four views (function, organization, data and control) and in all three phases (requirements definition, design specification and implementation).

The working result of the PPC ERM that has been developed forms the core of the data view. The process model for creating the PPC requirements definition data view is described in the function model, and the involvement of specific specialist departments and system analysts is recorded in the organization model. Additionally, the relationships between the components are established in the context of the requirements definition control view. A record is also made of which employees have specified given modellings in the course of which function. This makes it possible to record how versions of a data model or a function model are generated for an applications area.

Initially, each requirements definition for creating the data model can be created as a requirements definition without reference to the support tools (quasi with paper and pencil). These steps are indicated in Fig. A.V.04 by diagonal shading. The requirements definitions can then be modified in light of the design tool requirements (design specification), so that it can then be implemented in the repository with a special tool (implementation phase).

These steps are indicated by vertical shading in Fig. A.V.04.

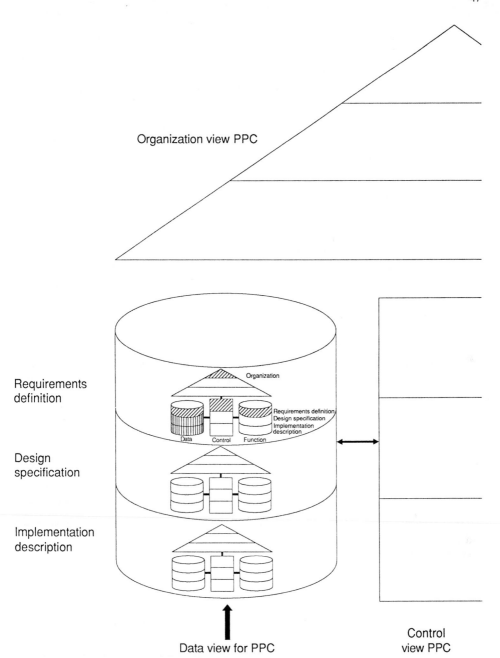

Organization view PPC

Requirements definition

Design specification

Implementation description

Organization

Requirements definition
Design specification
Implementation description

Data    Control    Function

Data view for PPC

Control view PPC

Fig. A.V.04: Creation of the requirements definition for the data views of a PPC system

48

In summary:

1.    The ARIS architecture developed for describing an information system determines the procedural model for developing the information system.

2.    Since the procedural model can itself be regarded as an application it can also be described by the same architectural views just like any other applications system.

3.    The results of each process in the procedural model are described in the data view and stored in the repository.

4.    The determining factor for the storage of the results, that is, the conceptual database scheme for the function, data, organization and control models developed, is the database scheme of the repository, in other words, the meta-structure developed for the information system.

Fig. A.V.05 initially expresses this interdependence between the procedural model and the modelling of the applications information system in general graphical form. Fig. A.V.06 relates this to the example introduced for a PPC system. This follows on from Fig. A.III.02.

The basic structure of the procedural model of level 2 is generated from the architecture developed for level 3. Of course, it can be described in greater detail and extended using special structuring relationships (overlaps, parallels).

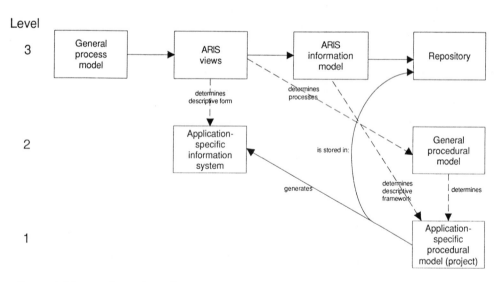

Fig. A.V.05: Interdependence between ARIS structure and procedural model

An application-specific procedural model, the execution of an individual project, is an instance of the general procedural model for creating an information system. This project management thus occurs at level 1.

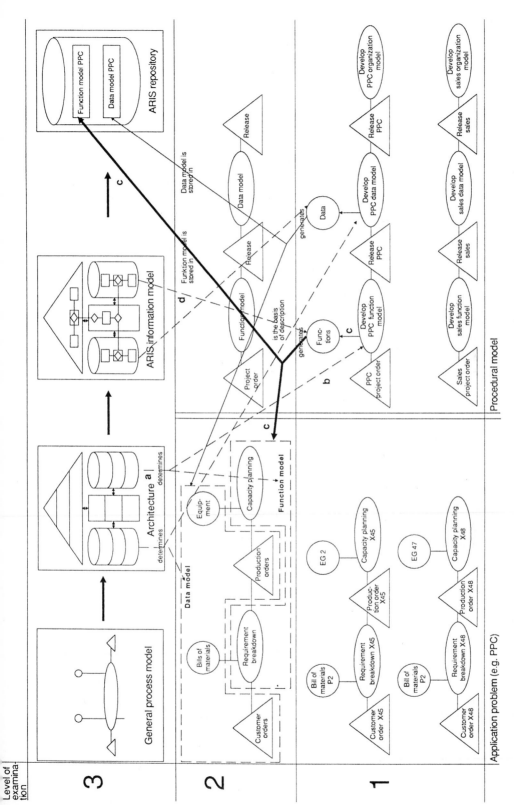

Fig. A.V.06: Interdependence between ARIS structure and the procedural model for PPC example introduced

The broken arrows indicate how the meta-level determines the lower levels, and the unbroken arrows give the results of the procedural model. The arrows are labelled using lower case letters.

The process "development of PPC function model" derives from the ARIS architecture (arrow a) and generates the function model at level 2 of the PPC applications area (arrow b). This is stored as an instance in the function model repository of level 3 (arrow c). The basis for the procedural description here is the process meta-model, in which the objects to be described and the kind of relationships between them are established (arrow d). This covers the extent to which processes can be broken down, interwoven or amalgamated to larger processes. This is extracted from the function information model.

The process "development of PPC data model" analogously generates the data structure of the PPC system, which is stored in the repository. These arrow links can also be interpreted as analogous to the function model.

## A.VI  Structure of the Remainder of the Book

### A.VI.1  Organizational Principle

In the following Part B the ARIS architecture that has been developed will be elaborated further into a comprehensive ARIS information model. The contents of the individual blocks will be described in more detail and design support procedures presented.

Thus, problem areas at level 2 of Fig A.III.02 will be considered and based on these objects and relationships for the meta-information model at level 3 will be derived. The complete ARIS information model accompanies this book as a fold-out (Fig. B.V).

Since many of the design methods form the basis of the information model it is correspondingly complex.

If a fixed methodical procedure was assumed from the start, conformity in the contents between terms at different phases could be more strictly defined, for example. As a result, an entity type from a higher phase could be adopted as the starting point for the consideration of the next phase. With a flexible approach, however, a new phase-specific term must be introduced which is merely linked with the first term via a relationship type.

The structure of the treatment follows the components of the architecture developed. The primary structuring criterion is that of the phases of the procedural model:

- process chain analysis (recording the semantic starting position),
- requirements definition,
- design specification, and
- implementation description.

In the process chain analysis the contents of the process chains are not yet broken down into views.

Thereafter, the three other phases are each broken down, according to the architectural views:

- functions,
- organization,
- data, and
- control.

As well as describing the content of an architectural block, for example how the requirements definition of the function view of an applications system can be represented, the creation of this requirements definition can itself also be described. This generates a "procedural model for creating the requirements definition of the function view" of an application system.

Given the close relationships between the creation of an architectural block and the description of its results each section will consider the associated procedural model. Since the creation itself represents an application, it is described using the same architecture.

This means that in each section a complete procedural model constructed according to the ARIS architectural principles can be described for the component under consideration. This means, in addition, that for the process "creation of the design specification for the data view", for example, requirements definitions for the functions, organization, data and control of the factors involved in the creation would need to be generated, and the design specification through to implementation would need to be generated therefrom. This means that 4 x 3 = 12 sub-sections would be required. This would impede the clarity of the presentation.

Therefore, in Part B the procedural models are considered simply for the requirements definitions. This is justified by the fact that the procedural models display considerable similarity and can therefore be easily transferred to the other levels.

Furthermore, within the procedural models it is not the phases that are chosen as the principal structuring criterion, but the views, and within one view the issues relating to the requirements definition, design specification and implementation are considered together.

In the course of explaining the design specification and the implementation description, issues relating to the use of tools for creating information systems are also considered.

In each individual section the subject matter currently being considered is illustrated using the architectural outline of Fig. A.II.04 in order to provide orientation for the reader.


## A.VI.2 Extending the Descriptive Language

The Entity-Relationship Model is of significance in two ways within this book. It serves first as a general descriptive language for all meta-models, and second as a descriptive language for the semantic data models of the applications systems at level 2.

This also means that the Entity-Relationship Model for data modelling can itself be represented at the meta-level as an entity relationship model.

The Entity-Relationship Model has been further developed since its creation by Chen (see *Chen, Entity-Relationship Model 1976*). Some of these further developments have been adopted in the following descriptions.

Generalization/Specialization
Entity types can be specialized into sub-entity types or generalized into a higher level entity type (see Fig. A.VI.01).


Grouping
In grouping, several elements of an entity type are amalgamated into groups. These groups are instances of a new entity type. In Fig. A.VI.02 employees are grouped together into departments. The entity type DEPARTMENT contains the individual departments as instances and has its own attributes. This operator is described by a 1:n relationship between DEPARTMENT and EMPLOYEE.


Reinterpretation of relationship types into entity types
It is permissible for terms initially introduced as relationship types in subsequent design steps to become in turn the starting point for other relationships (see Fig. A.VI.03). To do this, they are reinterpreted as entity types. The key attributes of the relationship type are passed on to the new entity type, and from there to the relationship types associated with this entity type. This operation has already been used in Fig. A.III.01.

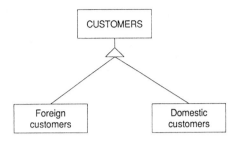

Fig A.VI.01: Generalization/specialization

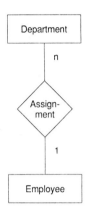

Fig. A.VI.02: Grouping

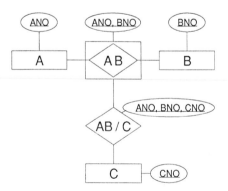

Fig. A.VI.03: Reinterpretation of a relationship type as an entity type

Cardinalities

The number of permissible and possible instances of a relationship for an entity type has thus far been expressed simply by the cardinalities 1 and n. In the following treatment a more exact representation will be introduced in the form of (min.-max.) notation. This means that from the viewpoint of an entity type to a relationship type the minimum and maximum permissible instances of the relationships belonging to the entity type are indicated on the relevant edge between the entity type and the relationship type being considered. Possible cases are presented in the first column of Fig. A.VI.04. An example is given in Fig. A.VI.05.

A department must have at least one employee assigned to it, but it may also have n (i.e. as many as desired). In contrast, an employee can be assigned to only one department. An employee may be assigned to no sub-projects or to many. However, a sub-project must be assigned at least one employee, but it could be as many as desired. A project must consist of at least one sub-project, but there may be several; a sub-project, however, is assigned to precisely one project.

The notation given in the second column of Fig. A.VI.04 is also used for the (min.-max.) expressions.

The "less precise" notation, specifying only 1 and n is given in the third column. In this case the 1 can signify that 0 is also permissible, whereas it may also mean that 1 is the lower limit.

For reasons of simplicity, other books from this author have frequently used the notation in the third column.

Existential/identificatory dependence

Fig. A.VI.05 contains two further representational elements. The existential dependence of an entity type indicates that it can only exist in conjunction with another entity type. For instance, the entity type EMPLOYEE only makes sense when the entity type DEPARTMENT has been defined.

Since the (min.-max.) notation requires that each employee must be assigned to one department, the converse also applies that the term DEPARTMENT only makes sense when the entity type EMPLOYEE also exists, and thus a lower limit of 1 also exists.

In addition to existential dependence, one also speaks of identificatory dependence (see *Knolmayer/Myrach, Tools zur Darstellung und Analyse von Datenmodellen, 1990 p. 95*) if an entity type can only be identified by the key attribute of another entity type. This occurs in the case of the entity-type SUB-PROJECT which is identified by the key attribute project number in combination with the assignment of a current number for each of the sub-projects within a project. This is indicated by a double line around the entity type.

In the entity relationship model, existentially dependent entity types are referred to as weak entity types. Knolmayer is right in pointing out the difference between existential and identificatory dependence and restricts the double line to the latter case. However, this semantic refinement is hardly needed in the following treatment.

| min, max | 1, c, m-Notation | "imprecise" 1, n-Notation |
|----------|------------------|---------------------------|
| 1, 1 | 1 | 1 |
| 0, 1 | c | 1 |
| 1, n | m | n |
| 0, n | m c | n |

Fig. A.VI.04: Cardinality notation

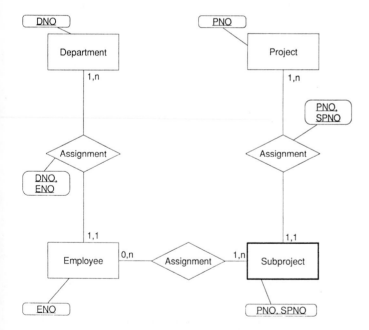

Fig. A.VI.05: Existential and identificatory dependence

## B. Development of the ARIS Information Model (Meta-Information System)

### B.I Process Chain Analysis (Recording the Semantic Starting Position)

Before the individual blocks (views) of an information system can be modelled, the semantic starting position must be available. This contains the goals to be pursued by the information system, the weaknesses of the existing system that are to be eliminated, and the essential features of the planned concept of the system to be developed. As many factors as possible from the function, organization and data areas, including the interdependences existing between them, need to be recorded, so that they can be formalized and further refined in the subsequent steps.

The fundamental influence of information technology on organizational processes is obvious above all by the consistent support for process chains. The integrative principle has given rise to comprehensive EDP-oriented sector-specific concepts. An EDP-oriented applications concept indicates how the strict use of information and communication technology can eliminate the weak points in the existing situation and how a new concept should be structured (see Fig. B.I.01). This is associated with the term CIM (Computer Integrated Manufacturing) in industrial firms, with the term retail information and control systems for trading firms, and with the term electronic banking for banking firms (see *Scheer, Principles of Efficient Information Management 1991* and *Scheer, CIM 1991*). This type of sector-specific concept must then be consolidated into concrete individual projects for an enterprise-specific system structuring. For example, from the CIM concept applying to an entire industrial enterprise a special project can be selected to speed up product development or introduce an integrated online production control system.

To do this, an analysis of current weaknesses is undertaken with the involvement of the specialist departments concerned, and a rough planned concept generated, taking the information technology possibilities into account. Given the long term commitment to the concept, it is not the effects of individual hardware or software products that are considered, but development trends such as networking possibilities, the use of databases, decentralization of hardware and software, and the applications software available.

The planned concept thus developed must be specified in sufficient detail to permit choices between competing projects and economic feasibility analyses; furthermore, once an implementation decision has been made, it should serve as a starting point for further modelling. It should thereby specify the boundaries of the area to be considered and the semantic factors should provide the starting point for the detailed modelling. The breakdown into views, in accordance with the architecture introduced is thus effected only in the subsequent processing steps, with the development of the requirements definition. The right hand arrow in Fig. B.I.01 indicates that EDP-oriented business application concepts can also make demands on the further development of information and communication technology. This will not be considered further here, however. Nevertheless, they remain part of the concerns of EDP-oriented business administration.

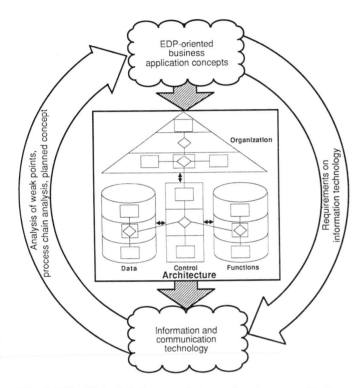

Fig. B.I.01: Mutual influences between business application concepts and information and communication technology

Given the requirement that the existing business application issues be described in all their complexity, the use of modelling procedures is limited. These tend to be developed later for the individual views. Fig. B.I.02 and B.I.03 present process chain diagrams for customer order processing and purchasing as examples of semi-formal procedures, which have also proved themselves useful in practical projects. A process chain diagram (see *Scheer, Principles of Efficient Information Management 1991*, pp. 35) represents a self-contained process chain. In the left column the individual processes are listed. The relationship to the organization is indicated by the details of the organizational unit (e.g. department) responsible for the process in the right hand column. This also includes external partners such as customers and suppliers. The intermediate columns indicate whether computer systems are used to handle the process, or whether manual processing predominates. Within these processing forms databases are indicated in general form, and within the computerized functions batch and interactive processing are distinguished.

Within a process chain diagram a situation analysis can show where there are media discontinuities between computerized and manual processing, and thus highlights the weak points of the current approach. In particular, data redundancy, multiple recording, and time delays within the process are visible. These weak points then provide suggestions for improvements in the planned concept. For example, this might be that more unified, consistent databases should be constructed to support more up-to-date and non-redundant processing, as suggested in the contrast between the two diagrams.

Process chain diagrams allow all the dimensions of the process chain model that have been discussed - organization, function, data and resource views, and the relationships between them - to be expressed in a unified form.

Software development methods, which are employed in the requirements definition phase, use special tools to represent their semantic starting position distinct from the actual descriptive language.

For the SA (Structured Analysis) descriptive procedure, this is obvious from the fact that the semantic starting position is described using so-called context diagrams with their own symbols. The actual procedure is applied at a lower level, whereby a top down approach with successive refinements can be implemented (see Fig. B.I.04). For a concrete example of a context diagram see *Balzert (ed.), CASE: Systeme und Werkzeuge 1989, p. 65.*

Given the restricted view of the SA diagrams in which essentially the data flow is represented, the view of the diagrams is narrower than that of the process chain diagram. But it could be extended to represent resources and organizational units.

In the first instance, the meta-structure of process chain diagrams will not be generated, since this would anticipate the meta-models of the individual views. It will, therefore, be elaborated in Section B.II.4, in which the individual views at the requirements definition level are amalgamated under the control section. At the same time, this should also indicate that process chains diagrams in detailed form are also suitable for representing

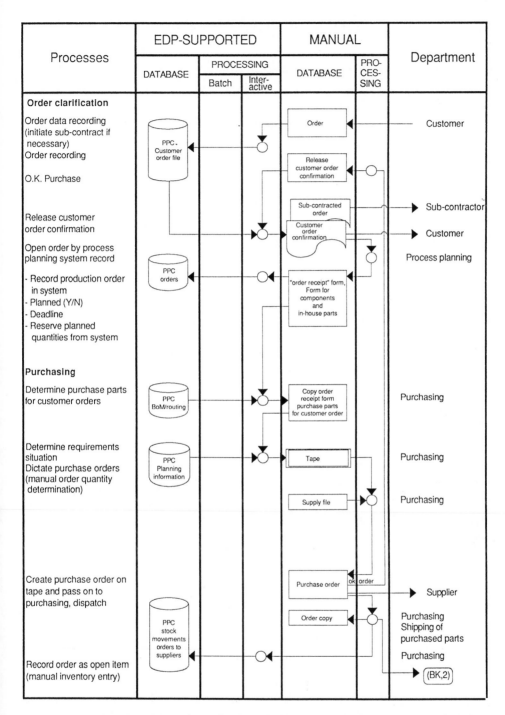

**Fig. B.I.02: Actual process of customer order processing and purchasing as a process chain diagram**

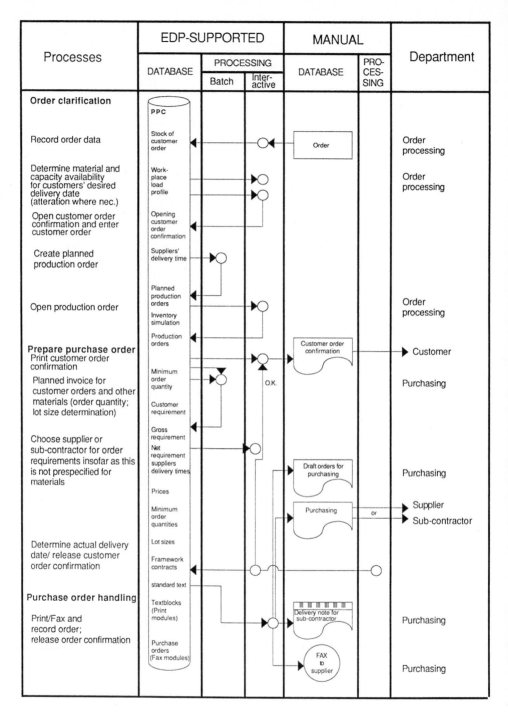

Fig. B.I.03: Planned process of customer order processing and purchasing as a process chain diagram

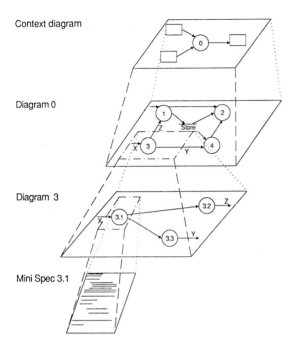

**Fig. B.I.04: SA hierarchy model**

from: *Balzert (ed.), CASE: Systeme und Werkzeuge 1989, p. 64*

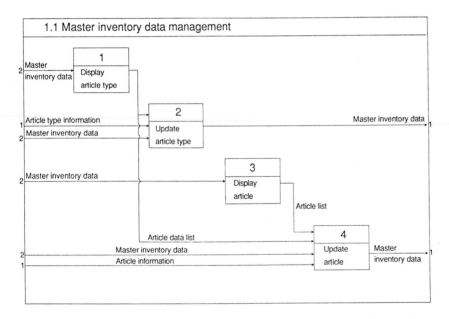

**Fig. B.I.05: Object flow diagram for representing the semantic starting position**

from: *Stucky/Nemeth/Schönthaler, INCOME 1989, p. 194*

the requirements definition level, and thus the transition between the starting position and the level at which the requirements definitionis determined is fluid.

The INCOME concept developed by Stucky et al. of a comprehensive applications development on the basis of Petri nets also uses a special procedure to represent the semantic starting point. The object flow diagram they use (see Fig. B.I.05) first considers data and processes together. In the subsequent modelling process they are separated, whereby static structures are represented with the help of object structure diagrams and behavioural aspects with the help of predicate transition nets.

## B.II Modelling the Requirements Definition

Once the semantic starting position has been established by the process chain analysis, in the following design phases it is considered separately from the various architectural viewpoints.

The formal description of the requirements definition is referred to as modelling. Correspondingly, the results of the section "modelling of the requirements definitions" are function, organization, data and control models.

They provide the starting point for the subsequent translation into design specifications and their ultimate implementation. The term modelling is used to express the idea that languages are employed permitting a level of formality of representation which allows the models to be transformed as automatically as possible in the subsequent phases of the development process.

In each case, the meta-model is developed from the description of the functional contents of the individual blocks. If individual sub-sections are formed within the description, the meta-model of the block is amalgamated at the end of the block description.

Following the representation of the contents of a block, the procedural model of the modelling process is investigated. This means that each modelling is treated within the components of the architecture. Of course, not all aspects are considered at the same level of detail. Consequently, a detailed breakdown according to all criteria is superfluous. The foreground is occupied by the analysis according to the four architectural blocks (views), whereby, within blocks, the design specification, that is, the use of modelling support tools, occupies the foreground.

## B.II.1  Requirements Definition of the Function View

### B.II.1.1  Function Description

As yet, no uniform descriptive language has been developed for the description of functions. Often, functions are described in association with other architectural blocks. This applies particularly to the link between functions and data, since functions describe the information transformation process, that is, they transform input data into output data. But functions are also described in association with organization objects, particularly from the communication viewpoint.

In the ARIS architecture, however, a strict separation of the architectural blocks is adopted in the first instance. Functions are considered from the viewpoint of their breakdown (function structure), their processing sequence, and their support using decision models.

Here, the description of these interdependences occupies the foreground. The optimization of function processes, e. g. using simulation techniques, is considered below (see Section B.II.1.2.1).

There is no generally applicable definition of the term "function". Here, it is regarded as largely synonymous with the term "process". Process chains are thus not contrary to the term "function", but rather a combination of functions. The symbols for representing functions also lack uniformity. Fig. B.II.01 summarizes some of the more commonly used symbols for function representation. Here, an oval will be used.

The categorization of the function block is represented in Fig. B.II.02. The basis for the function modelling is the EDP-oriented business application concept. Here, the goals which the functions are intended to support are defined. Goals can be derived from the concept of critical success factors developed by Rockart (see *Rockart, Critical Success Factors 1982*).

A function can then be defined as an operation carried out on an object with the aim of supporting one or more goals. A detailed summary of goals and functions is given by J. Martin (see *Martin, Information Engineering, Planning and Analysis 1990, p. 77*). Goals can be interdependent (see Fig. B.II.03). In addition, one sub-goal can support several primary goals (goal 02.2 with respect to goals 01 and 02). The structure of the goals, which are linked together in a kind of network, thus forms an n:m relationship within the entity type ENTERPRISE GOALS (see Fig. B.II.04). To differentiate the two edges between ENTERPRISE GOALS and GOAL STRUCTURE they are assigned role names. Since the

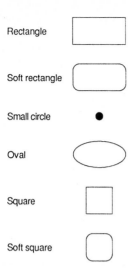

Rectangle

Soft rectangle

Small circle

Oval

Square

Soft square

Fig. B.II.01: Symbols for function representation

from: *Olle/Hagelstein/MacDonald, Information Systems, p. 199*

primary goals cannot be assigned to any other higher level goals, whereas sub-goals can be assigned to several (n) goals, the "higher level" edge has a cardinality in the min.-max. notation of 0,n. The same cardinality applies to the "lower level" edge, since the lowest level of sub-goals cannot have any further goals below them.

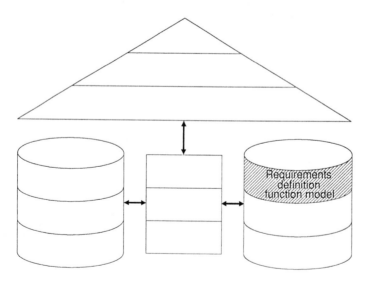

Fig. B.II.02: Incorporating the requirements definition functions in ARIS

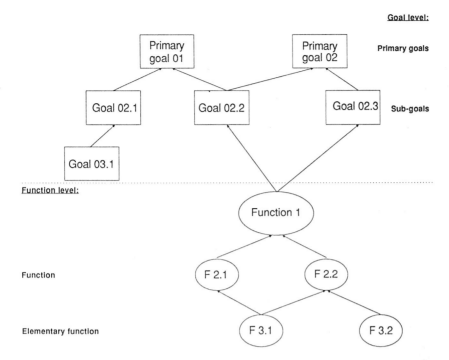

Fig. B.II.03: Goals and function structures

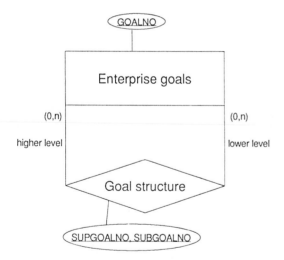

Fig. B.II.04: ERM for representing goal structures

### B.II.1.1.1 Function Structure

Functions can be described at various levels of consolidation. The highest level of consolidation, and hence the starting point for the analysis, are collections of functions in the form of business processes or process chains. They serve to provide direct support for enterprise goals. A process chain describes a complex operation from its origination through to its completion. For example, the processing of a customer order from the customer query through to dispatch is such a process, or the management of a project, e. g. the construction of a new plant, from planning through to its coming on stream. The criterion for defining a process is usually an object, in the above examples the customer order and the construction project.

A process, therefore, consists of related operations, which have many interconnections. In order to reduce the complexity, it is therefore structured, that is, it is broken down into sub-functions. This breakdown is represented using hierarchy diagrams (see Fig. B.II.05).

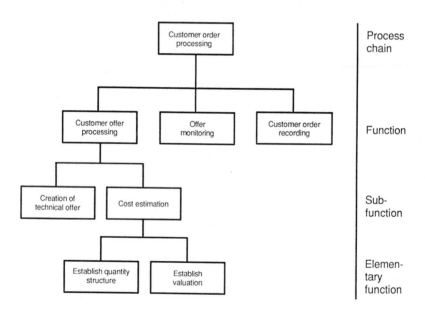

Fig. B.II.05: Example of a hierarchy diagram

In principle, the term function can be applied at all hierarchy levels. However, it is often broken down according to the level of detail of the analysis into:

| Process chain: | Object-related complex process. |
|---|---|
| Function: | Complex activity which can be further sub-divided, and enters directly into a process. |
| Sub-function: | Activity which can be broken down into further sub-functions or elementary functions, and enters into higher level functions. |
| Elementary function: | Activity which cannot be meaningfully further sub-divided. Criteria are the complete processing at one workplace, or an established procedural structure with no processing alternatives. |

These terms can only be distinguished from each other arbitrarily. Consequently, the following discussion merely distinguishes between the terms process and function, since they correspond to different defining properties (object-related and activity-related).

Although the breakdown of functions using hierarchy diagrams is widespread, the use of this top-down procedure is problematic. Clear rules for the breakdown procedure are not generally available, so that monitoring the consistency of the functions at a given level is difficult (see *Falkenberg/Nijssen/Adams, Feature Analysis 1983, p. 177*). In contrast, the reverse process of amalgamating elementary functions into larger functional units can be carried out more systematically. Consequently, practical applications should follow both methods: first, the functions are broken down in a top-down approach to obtain suggestions for elementary functions, then, these can be reconstructed in a bottom-up approach.

Instructive application examples for function hierarchies are given by J. Martin (see *Martin, Information Engineering, Planning and Analysis 1990, p. 45 ff.*, see also *Olle/Hagelstein/MacDonald, Information Systems 1988, p. 57*).

A function can enter into various higher level functions through to process chains. For example, the function "order acceptance" can be incorporated in the process chain for handling spare parts as well as the process chain for order handling for new business. The same applies to the function "availability check", which can be a component of the process chain for order processing, or for the release of production orders within production control.

If functions were only managed within a tree structure, considerable redundancy would arise. Therefore, the term "general function" is defined which describes activities independent of their process associations. The function "order acceptance" or "availability check" is thus defined only once as a general function. The term general function generates an entity type G-FUNCTION with the key attribute GFCTNO (see Fig. B.II.06). All the characteristics of the function which are independent of their incorporation in process environments are described as attributes of this entity type. Following the suggestion of Olle et al., a distinction can be drawn between the name of the elements introduced and the elements themselves, i. e. between the name of the general function and the general function itself (see *Olle/Hagelstein/MacDonald, Information Systems 1988*). In this way, synonyms and homonyms, which can also result from the inclusion of a multi-language concept, for example, can be handled easily. For reasons of simplicity, the following treatment will dispense with this representational effect, which is not to deny its importance.

Furthermore, the explicit representation of so-called "external processes" or "external agents" by their own entity types is also dispensed with. External processes generate links with operations which occur outside the area being modelled. Here, they are regarded as part of the general function terms and can easily be extracted by means of a specialization.

If a general function is included in a process chain then a relationship between the entity types PROCESS and G-FUNCTION is generated. The functions presented in the hierarchy diagram in Fig. B.II.05 are thus elements of the relationship type FUNCTION in Fig. B.II.06. The complex key "process number" PRNO and "general function number" GFCTNO makes this connection obvious. The relationship type FUNCTION can on the one hand take over (inherit) attributes of the general function via the relation, on the other hand the relationship type can be assigned further attributes relating to the process associations.

Processes support enterprise goals. This connectivity is generated by introducing the relationship type SUPPORT between PROCESS and ENTERPRISE GOALS. The cardinalities between PROCESS and GOALS and between G-FUNCTION and PROCESS each possess a lower limit of 1. A process which does not support any enterprise goal is pointless, as is a process which has no functions assigned to it.

The function structure of the hierarchy diagram can be generated via a relationship within the term FUNCTION which is reinterpreted as an entity type. The relationship type FUNCTION STRUCTURE is identified by specifying the higher level and lower level (complex) function key. The edges are provided with role names (higher level or lower level). Since a function can arise several times within a process, a net structure is represented, from which the tree structures can be derived. Functions at the highest level of the hierarchy enter directly into enterprise processes, and therefore have no higher level following function. Elementary functions at the lowest function level are not broken down further and therefore have no lower level following function. For this reason, the lower limits of the cardinalities are both 0.

Fig. B.II.07 presents an example of functional representation from the production planning and control process chain. The functions "availability check" and "reservation",

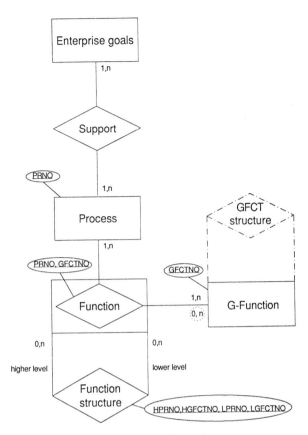

Fig. B.II.06: Function and goal structures

along with their subordinate functions, arise with reference both to medium term production planning in the order release context, and to short term production control in the operation release context.

The upper part of the figure shows the tree structure with its redundant functions, and the lower part the non-redundant network representation which is given by the data structure.

Differences between the description of functions can be expressed by attributes of the relationship type FUNCTION STRUCTURE.

If a function which arises at several points in the process chain needs to be individually identifiable, this can be represented by assigning role names (see Fig. B.II.08). A function is then identified by its role name, its process chain, and its fundamental meaning. Role names can also act as substitutes for other elements in the information system which have not yet been fully formulated. For example, in the case shown in Fig. B.II.07 it could

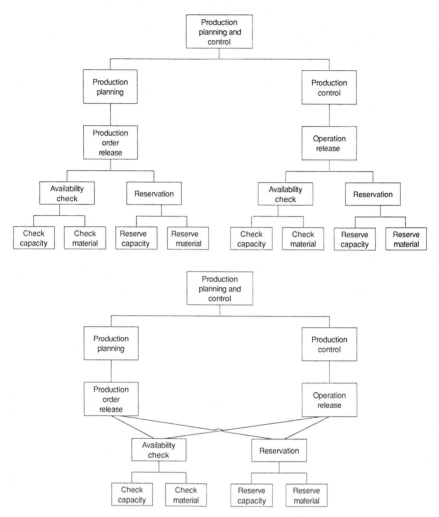

Fig. B.II.07: Example of function representation from the PPC process chain

substitute for the term "organizational unit", if the PPC process chain is distributed hierarchically over several organizational units, the medium term availability check being carried out at the factory level and the short term availability check is carried out at the departmental level.

The solution presented here allows each general function in a process association to retain special characteristics. In contrast, if functions are defined so precisely that they are handled identically in all applications contexts, and also consist of the same sub-functions, then it is appropriate to treat them as generic building blocks endowed with assignment relationships to their sub-functions, and then later simply to link these blocks to the processes. With respect to the data structure of Fig. B.II.06, this would mean that a relationship type GFCT-STRUCTURE would represent the block connections and the cardinality between G-FUNCTION and FUNCTION would be altered to (0,n), since now each general function does not need to be assigned to one process, but merely to the higher level block function. In Fig. B.II.06 this case is shown by the dotted representation. This discussion points the way to a possible representation of building blocks in the sense of the CIM-OSA architecture.

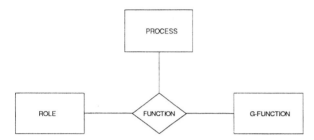

Fig. B.II.08: Assigning role names

## B.II.1.1.2  Operational Sequence

In addition to defining a function structure, it is also the task of the requirements definition to establish the operational sequence of functions. Here, no descriptive procedure has as yet gained wide acceptance. The concepts of network planning for project planning can provide comprehensive possibilities for describing processes. These not only represent differentiated predecessor and successor relationships, but also, by specifying intervals, overlaps and minimum gaps between processes. Furthermore, logical links between incoming and outgoing assignment relationships can be defined with respect to both the incoming and the outgoing side of processes. Fig. B.II.09 gives the sequence of an excerpt from the hierarchy tree representation. It shows, first, that the sequencing links cannot be derived from the hierarchy representation, but a new descriptive view needs to be introduced. On completion of the cost estimation, for which both the valuations (e. g. labour cost rates) and the quantity structure of the costs of the order are required, a decision node is depicted which has the following three alternatives as outputs: the creation of a new technical offer (since the cost estimation has led to an unrealistic price), the termination of the process on the basis of the assessment that a revision of the offer would be unsuccessful, or the recording of the order because the customer has accepted the offer. The proportions in which the various alternatives arise can be assigned as attributes to the edges. As mutually exclusive alternatives they must sum to 1.

This notation is based on the GERT (graphical evaluation and review technique) procedure (see *Elmaghraby, Activity Networks 1977*, see also *Scheer, Projektsteuerung 1978*).

With the help of Petri nets further refinements of the process logic can be represented (see *Reisig, Systementwurf mit Netzen 1985* and *Reisig, Petrinetze 1986*), see also the discussion of the control view of the requirements definitions below.

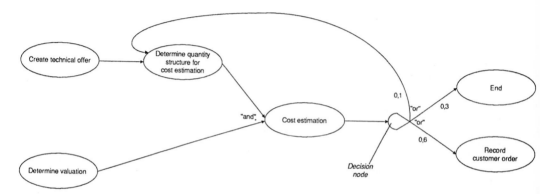

Fig. B.II.09: Process sequence of functions

The decision node introduced could, as an event occurring at a specific timepoint, constitute an independent representational element of the description. However, it is also possible to interpret it as process with a duration of 0.

In general, processes are defined as time-consuming entities (occurences), which begin with a starting event and finish with an end event. Consequently, each process always has two events associated with it which can also be the subject of decision considerations.

The decision nodes are thus either assigned to the end events of processes, or the decision-making is itself interpreted as a process. Both representational forms are shown in Fig. B.II.10.

Later, events will be given special treatment in the context of the control between data and functions.

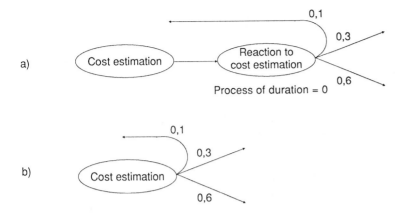

Fig. B.II.10: Alternative representation of decision nodes.

SEQUENCES constitute a new relationship type within the entity type FUNCTION. Each sequence relationship can be identified by specification of the preceding and following functional step. This is indicated in Fig. B.II.11 by the adoption of the first letter of the edge role. The instances of the sequence relationships, that is, the individual edges, can be assigned attributes to handle the intervals for overlaps or delays, or coefficients expressing the proportional values in the case of branching alternatives.

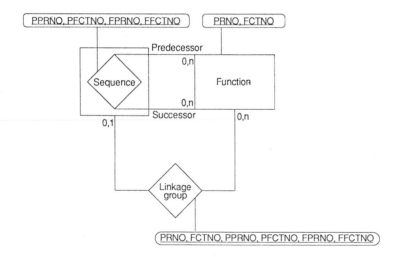

Fig. B.II.11: Handling of sequence relationships

The logical links between incoming and outgoing sequence relationships can be formulated, in that for each function the form in which the incoming edges for this process are linked, or in which form this applies to the outgoing edges which are established. If logical dependences are interpreted as characteristics of the edges, they can be assigned as attributes to the sequence relationships. In contrast, logical links between groups of incoming or outgoing sequence relationships require special representation. One possibility would be to construct a relationship between FUNCTION and SEQUENCE RELATIONSHIP reinterpreted as an entity type, which amalgamates a linkage group of sequence relationships. A sequence relationship can then be involved in at most one linkage group (see Fig. B.II.12).

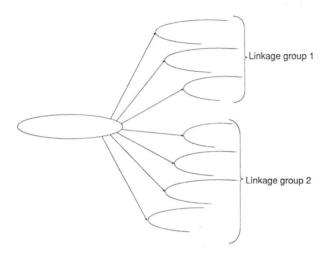

Fig. B.II.12: Linkage groups of sequence relationships

In the ERM representation, on the other hand, a non-redundant representation of functional interdependences is achieved. This means that a function is only featured once, even when it arises repeatedly in a process chain.

Important incoming and outgoing data are often specified in process descriptions. The data are not regarded as independent descriptive objects, however, as is the case in the ARIS data view in the form of the data model, for example, but merely promote a more accurate function representation.

These kind of data that are exchanged between functions can be assigned as attributes to the sequence relationships. If several attributes are needed between two processes, these can be identified by allocating a role entity type or a "counter entity type" which is linked with the relationship type.

As well as data, other characteristics, such as the exchange of physical objects (materials, capital, etc.), can be represented by attributes of the sequence relationships.

The function diagram of the SADT procedure or the IDEF0 method derived from it can

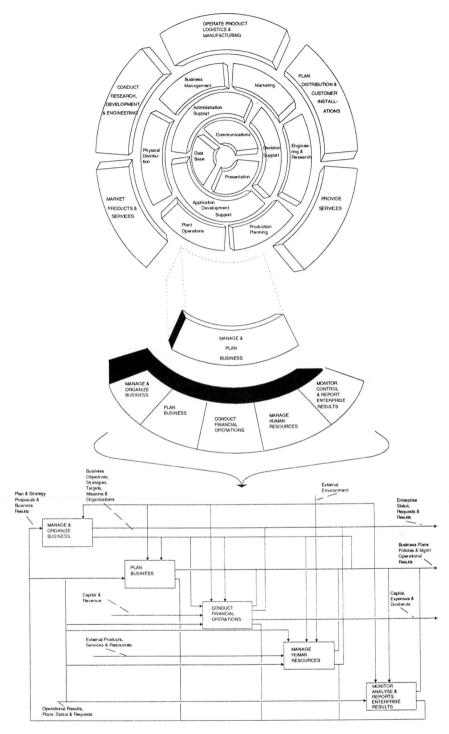

Fig. B.II.13: Manage and Plan Business

source: *IBM*

also be regarded as this kind of extended function representation. Fig. B.II.13 presents an excerpt from a CIM process model.

A function (activity) is represented by a box. The arrows entering from the left side characterize the input, which can include both information and physical input such as parts or materials. The output is characterized by the arrows leaving at the right, which can relate both to products, services, or flows of funds, and to information.

The arrows entering vertically from above characterize constraints on the function. The arrows entering vertically from below characterize the mechanisms (resources) used.

Fig. B.II.13 describes the function excerpt "Manage and Plan Business" of the CIM model using 5 sub-functions:

- manage (definition of management processes, policies and goals),
- plan, (transformation of management directives into specific plans),
- direct (transformation of the plans into instructions for action),
- operate (execution of the plans), and
- control (monitor the execution).

### B.II.1.1.3 Processing Forms

The functions have thus far been represented independent of their EDP support. To indicate whether a function is processed primarily by computer or by hand the specialized terms "SYSTEM FUNCTION" and "MANUAL FUNCTION" are introduced as specializations of the term G-FUNCTION (see Fig. B.II.14).

Examples of system functions are "setting up customer order", "maintenance of customer data" or "preparation of customer statistics".
The establishment of the general processing form for system functions also counts as part of the requirements definition. The essential criterion for the type of processing is whether a user can have a controlling influence on the process, or whether the process is executed without user interaction. The first case is referred to as interactive processing, the second as batch processing. Diverse criteria can be employed to assess whether a function is suited to interactive processing, as shown in Fig. B.II.15. The entity type SYSTEM FUNCTION is therefore broken down further into the sub-types USER TRANSACTION and BATCH RUN. The term USER TRANSACTION is here used in a very

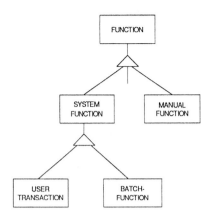

Fig. B.II.14: Specialization of the term function

general sense. It indicates the processing unit within which a unified task is processed interactively with user control. It should not be confused with the term database transaction which will be introduced later, and which is of greater implementation significance.

| Characteristics / Goals | Event-orientation (Currency) | Function integration (Plausibility) | Interacvtive decision-making | Avoidance of bottle-necks | Handling improve-ments | Qualitative improve-ments |
|---|---|---|---|---|---|---|
| Time savings | x | x | x | x | x | |
| Personnel savings | | x | | x | x | |
| Informational gains | x | | x | | | x |
| Job satisfaction | x | x | | x | x | x |
| Simplification of organizational procedures | | x | x | | x | |

Fig. B.II.15: Criteria and goals of interactive processing

from: *Scheer, Principles of Efficient Information Management 1991, p. 77*

### B.II.1.1.4 Decision Models

Information systems are not only employed to support the functional interdependences of operational structures, but also as decision-making support. An example might be where an optimization method is used to determine the optimal production plan in the production planning context.

To make the discussion more concrete a linear programming (LP) model is assumed as a typical example of the structure of a decision model. In an LP model the variables are specified in accordance with side conditions such that an objective function is maximized (see Fig. B.II.16).

An LP model thus consists of the elements VARIABLE, EQUATION (in the form of side conditions and objective function) and COEFFICIENT.

The entity type DECISION MODEL is specified for the individual decision models (see Fig. B.II.17). Within one function (e. g. production planning) several decision models can be employed; conversely, one decision model can also be used for several different applications, the differences being determined by the different data sets. For this reason, the cardinalities are of type (0,n).

Goal function: $$\sum_j c_j x_j \longrightarrow max$$

Side conditions: $$\sum_j a_{ij} x_j \leq A_i \text{ , for all } i$$

$$x_j \geq 0 \text{ , for all } j$$

Variables: $x_j$
Coefficients: $a_{ij}$

Fig. B.II.16: Structure of an LP model

One decision model is assigned several equations, whereby one equation can occur in various models (e. g. a capacity side condition in a model for short term production planning and in a model for investment planning). The VARIABLES introduced as entity types can also be employed in several decision models. Examples of variables are output levels, sales levels, amounts invested, etc.

The links between the variables (columns of the LP matrix) and the equations (lines of the LP matrix) are generated by the coefficients. In the process, several equations can be provided with coefficients in one column (i. e. per variable), and conversely, several variables can be involved in one line (equation).

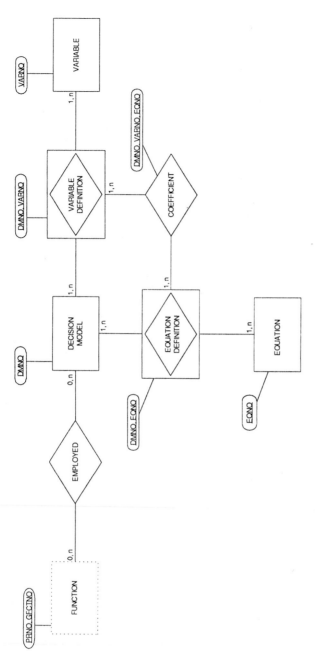

Fig. B.II.17: Logical structure of decision models.

Using matrix generators variables, equations and coefficients of a model can be generated from a database, in which all permissible index combinations of a variable can be defined from the logical link that is stored there (see *Scheer, Enterprise-Wide Data Modelling*

*1989, p. 402).* The MPS (Mathematical Programming System) format provides a widely standardized descriptive form.

The logical structure of decision models represented in Fig. B.II.17 can be filed in the repository in the form of a model bank of the individual models (see *Scheer, Principles of Efficient Information Management 1991, p. 149).*

The information objects introduced, EQUATION, VARIABLE and COEFFICIENT, contain primarily their definition and description in the context of the development model (e. g. their index marks and dimensions). The provision of data from an applications database will be considered in Section B.II.4 "Requirements Definition of the Control View".
As well as decision models of the LP type, other approaches such as simulation models and expert systems can be drawn upon to establish a meta-structure for decision support.

### B.II.1.1.5  The Requirements Definition Function Model

The models developed for the requirements definition of the functions are amalgamated into a complete model in Fig. B.II.18.

### B.II.1.2  The Procedural Model for Function Modelling (Requirements Definition)

Information processing can be regarded as an applications area just like production planning and control or sales. Since information systems can be employed to support information processing they can also be described within the ARIS architecture. This means that an information system supporting the block "requirements definition of function view" can be described from the four views and in the phases of the procedural model. In this sense, the procedural model is an application example demonstrating the meta-structure and descriptive constructs that have been developed.
The procedural model is also of significance as a result of its links with the results it produces, that is, the function model of an applications area. By way of the relationships between the procedural model and its results, versions of the applications descriptions can be documented and assigned to their development projects. This connection is considered in the section "Control View of the Procedural Model" and generates an extension to the meta-structure.

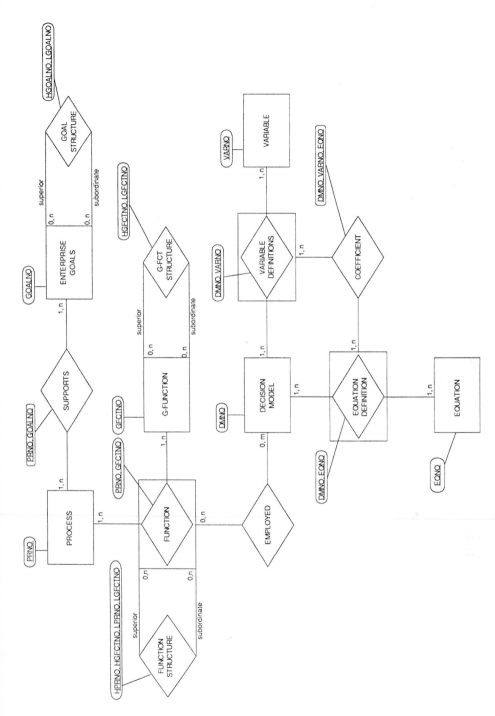

Fig. B.II.18: The requirements definition function model as an ERM

So as not to inflate the number of sections, only the four views (architectural blocks) are used as sub-headings. The various phases are then handled within one view.

One difficulty arises from the fact that blocks will be considered whose meta-structure has not yet been developed. As a result, the corresponding treatment is kept very general and largely verbal. Of course, they can then be independently incorporated in the meta-structure later, once they have been discussed.

### B.II.1.2.1 Function View of the Procedural Model for Function Modelling

The architectural element being considered within the block: requirements definition of the function view, is indicated by the shading in Fig. B.II.19.

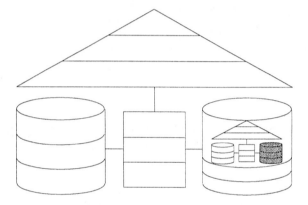

Fig. B.II.19: Function view of the procedural model for the requirements definition function view

Fig. B.II.20 represents a **requirements definition** for the functional procedure of function modelling with a hierarchy diagram and a process graph. Fig. B.II.21 gives a process list for the SADT procedure as an example of function modelling. The examples are self-explanatory and, since they use representative forms that have already been introduced, they can be incorporated in the meta-structure of the "requirements definition function model".

In elaborating a requirements definition for the function description computer tools such as graphic systems, or development tools such as IEW, msp-Easy, etc., can provide support. In the context of the **design specification** of the procedural model the descriptive elements are oriented towards the tool interfaces. Since tools are themselves

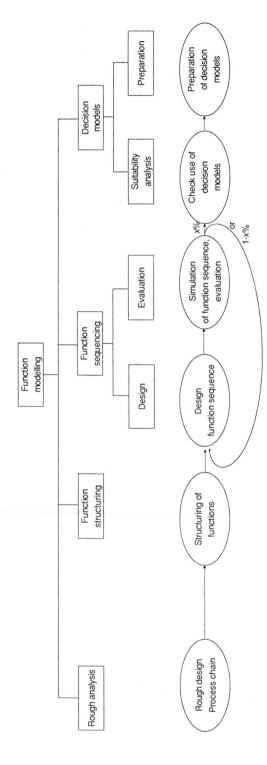

Fig. B.II.20: Requirements definition of the function view in the procedural model for function modelling (hierarchy diagram and function sequence)

oriented towards certain method definitions, this means that the requirements definition design needs to be adapted more closely to those methods in the function modelling which are supported by tools.

The EDP-supported representation of hierarchy diagrams scarcely requires adaptation. Almost all Case Tools offer appropriate graphically-oriented data representation possibilities.

Activities model

| | |
|---|---|
| 1 | Collect information. |
| 2 | Classify by activity and data and create activity lists |
| 3 | Establish perspective; several models can be developed for different perspectives, e.g. from the perspective of user groups 1,2, etc. |
| 4 | Establish aims: e.g. actual analysis of an existing system, or defining the requirements on a new system. |
| 5 | Establish interfaces with the environment using A-O diagrams. |
| 6 | Develop A-O diagram, max. 4-6 activities. Step 5 and 6 can be interchanged or carried out simultaneously. |
| 7 | Enter references between AO and A-O diagram |
| 8 | Refine AO using further diagrams (A1 ... An, n <= 6) |
| 9 | Repeat steps 7 and 8 until an adequate level of detail is achieved. |
| 10 | Draw up node index and glossary. |

Fig. B.II.21: Procedural model SADT (excerpt)

see: *Balzert, Die Entwicklung von Software-Systemen 1982, p. 128*

In the process chain analysis context tools can be employed which are still heavily based on the conceptual framework of business administration. In the "CIM Analyser" project (see *Jost/Keller/Scheer, Konzeption eines DV-Tools im Rahmen der CIM Planung 1991*) a tool is being developed which also supports the creation of application function concepts. The concept is heavily based on Scheer's Y-CIM model (see *Scheer, CIM 1991, p. 2*), so that definition conventions need to be taken into account here.

The tool CAPSIM (*Krcmar, Gestaltung von "Computer-am-Arbeitsplatz"-Systemen 1983; Scheer, Principles of Efficient Information Management 1991, p. 41*) and the tool from

Krallmann (see *Krallmann/Scholz-Reiter, CIM-KSA 1990, p. 57 ff.*) allow the simulation and optimization of process structures. Their entry interface is graphically-oriented and similar to the functional representation chosen here. For instance, branchings with their proportions are also possible. If the tools available only allow representation by conventional network plans, then branchings are not possible and must be removed from the description in the context of the design specification.

To support the development of decision models the so-called MPS notation is employed as interface with the definition of the model structure for LP models (see here e. g. *Scheer, Principles of Efficient Information Management 1991, p. 146 ff; Schmitz/Schönlein, Optimierungsmodelle 1978*).

An example of EDP-supported function recording is given in Fig. B.II.22 from the viewpoint of the CIM-OSA approach. The function definition, however, is not congruent with the definition used here. In particular, links to the other views are also recorded. Typical functions that can be supported by tools such as PREDICT CASE (see *Software AG (eds.), PREDICT CASE Einführung 1988, p. 5*) are data recording and maintenance, retrieval, evaluation and quality assurance. Functions for data recording and maintenance can be defined, renamed and deleted. In the retrieval context functions can be sought using attributes or name components from the function database. As

### Business Process

| | |
|---|---|
| Type : | [relevant category - select from list] |
| Identifier: | [relation to other business processes] |
| Name: | [name of business process] |
| Responsible: | [name of responsible entity (person, etc.)] |
| Comprises: | [list of business processes or enterprise activities used] |
| | |
| FUNCTION: | [short textual description of the task performed by the business process] |
| EVENT: | [name of enterprise event that triggers the activation of the business process] |
| RESULT: | [ name of business result that the business process creates] |
| PROCEDURAL RULE: | [name of procedural rule set (same name as business process] |
| DECLARATIVE RULE: | [name of declarative rule] |

Fig. B.II.22: CIM-OSA construct for recording business processes

from: *ESPRIT Consortium AMICE (eds.), Open System Architecture 1989, p. 104*

evaluations, functions can be represented in various forms, including function trees, for example (see Fig. B.II.23). Quality assurance can ensure that function sequences are internally consistent, that no impermissible cycles arise and that the predecessor/successor relationships are consistent.

The tools mentioned are generally available as standard software. Questions of **implementing** the tools are therefore mainly concerned with discussion of the hardware and system software environment which allows diverse tools to be linked together in a computer-technical sense. These issues, as well as the care of the run-time version, are not considered further here.

```
 13:09:27                ***** PREDICT CASE *****              30 - 09 - 87

 Plan 5                     - Management function -               XOOTRG1A

        Object name:     .bORDER ENTRY          Work status
 ----------------------------------- < Tree FU > ---------------------- Line 1

    F     Object name:     ORDER ENTRY_____Level:   9

    _        ORDER ACCEPTANCE
    _        :   NEW ORDER
    _        :   AMENDED ORDER
    _        :   CANCELLED ORDER
    _        ORDER CHECKING
    _        :   EXPORT AUTHORIZATION
    _        :   CREDIT CHECK
    _        :   AVAILABILITY CHECK
    _        ORDER CONFIRMATION
    _        :   SINGLE ORDER CONFIRMATION
    _        :   BATCH ORDER CONFIRMATION

    _
    _
    _

 Command: _____          ALL
 REL-PF1---PF2---PF3---PF4---PF5---PF6---PF7---PF8---PF9---PF10---PF11---PF12------
         ?   Menu Quit COmm +B   +K   V PL  PLan Next LOG  LAST
```

Fig. B.II.23: Management of functions using PREDICT-CASE (tree structure)

from: *Software AG (eds.), PREDICT CASE Einführung 1988, pp. 5-8*

### B.II.1.2.2 Organization View of the Procedural Model for Function Modelling

The incorporation of this section is shown in Fig. B.II.24. The function view already considered is dotted, the organization view is shaded.

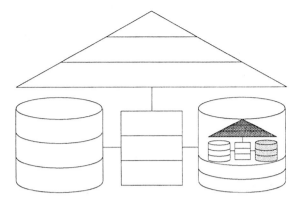

Fig. B.II.24: Incorporation of the function and organization view of the procedural model for function modelling

The **requirements definition** of the organization view concerns the project organization for creating a requirements definition for functions (see Fig. B.II.25). It is normal to establish a reference group which is reported to by the project leader. Various working groups for creating the function architecture for sub-areas are assigned to the project leader.

As well as undertaking the computerized management of the project organization (participants, areas of responsibility), the **design specification** establishes a concept for project control. Here, rules and representational elements of project control systems, such as MS-Project or Havard Total Project Manager (see *Kurbel/Dornhoff, Ein Projektmanagementsystem für evolutionäre Softwareentwicklungen 1990*, for example) need to be taken into account. If the project participants are spatially distributed a concept for their networking must be developed.

The implementation relates to the concrete execution of the project organization developed, using hardware and software components.

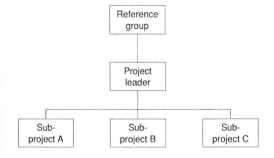

Fig. B.II.25: Organization view of the procedural model for function modelling

### B.II.1.2.3  Data View of the Procedural Model for Function Modelling

In Fig. B.II.26 the data view is shaded and the views already discussed are dotted.

In the requirements definition the objects and their relationships to each other are described, which are involved as frames of reference or events in the creation of the requirements definition function model.

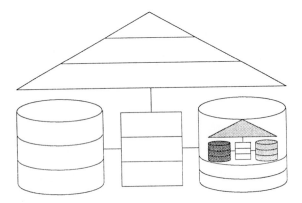

Fig. B.II.26: Incorporation of the data view of the procedural model for function modelling.

This connectivity is roughly represented in Fig. B.II.27. The function "create function model" is initiated by a project order and concluded by the event project completion.

In the creation of the function model documents concerning function descriptions are received which are altered or extended in the course of processing. The data view thus describes the milestones of the procedural model as well as the functions elaborated. These functions are stored in the repository.

The accompanying data model of the functions largely corresponds to the meta-structure developed for describing the functions (see Fig. B.II.18).

At the same time, this meta-model of functions provides the framework for the descriptive constructs available for the functions.

This is particularly effective in the course of elaborating the **design specification**. Here, the interfaces with the tools for function description and their data concepts must be taken into account.

The **implementation** is again very closely linked with the standard tools to be employed, and is not considered further here.

Data view

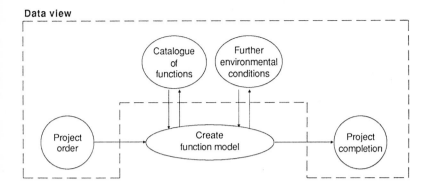

Fig. B.II.27: Data view of the procedural model for function modelling

## B.II.1.2.4  Control View of the Procedural Model for Function Modelling

In the control view the function, organization and data views of the procedural model are linked together (see Fig. B.II.28).

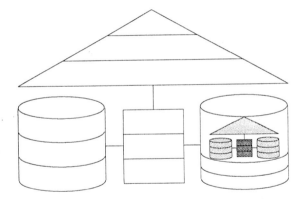

Fig. B.II.28:  Incorporation of the control view of the procedural model for function modelling

The meta-structure of this interdependence is given in rough form in Fig. B.II.29. First, the relationship type VERSIONS generates the link between a certain project for creating a function model and the function structures of the applications area thereby generated. In this way, various function models for the same application area can be managed with reference to particular development projects. The link between the act of generating a function during the project and the function itself can be established in detail by the relationship type PARTICIPANT or CREATED. These relationship types represent the assignment of the project team members to the phases of the procedural model.

At the level of the **design specification** the interfaces between the tools used in the individual views must be linked together. This means, for example, that a tool supporting the graphical representation of function sequences is compatible with the definition of function objects stored in the database.

At the **implementation level** the concrete computer tools must be compatible, and made available via a uniform development network to all the users involved.

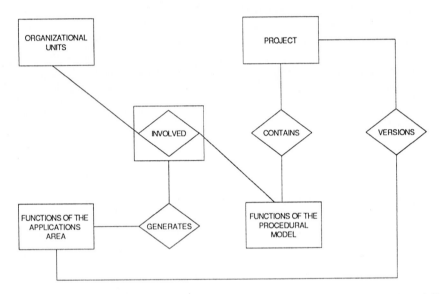

Fig. B.II.29: Linking the procedural model with the result of the function modelling

## B.II.2  Requirements Definition of the Organization View

The block for organization modelling is shown in shading in Fig. B.II.30. The block for function modelling already considered is dotted.

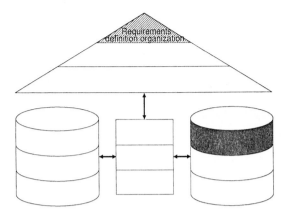

Fig. B.II.30: Incorporation of the requirements definition organization in ARIS

### B.II.2.1 Organization Description

Organizational units are the units responsible for the tasks to be supported by the information system.

The formation of organizational units is not the task of the information system, but rather of the business application functions "organization" or "personnel management". Here, criteria are defined in accordance with which the organizational units are formed, e. g. functional units, decision hierarchies, managerial authority. Of course, there are close links between information processing and the optimization of organizational structures, since information systems are used to support organizational processes.

In describing the organization or personnel management application area, the data structure is, therefore, considerably more differentiated and wide-ranging than the view adopted here (see e. g. Heilmann, *Organisationsinformationssystem 1989* or *Scheer, Enterprise-Wide Data modelling 1989, pp. 423*). Nevertheless, there are overlaps between the organization view of the ARIS architecture and the organization description from the application view.

Apart from their responsibility for functions and data, organizational units are also of significance for information systems as creators and users of the information system. The users are addressees of the user interface of the information system. The developers of an information system have been considered in the context of the organization view of the procedural model (see Fig. B.II.29).

### B.II.2.1.1 Organizational Structure

Organization structures are represented by organizational charts (see Fig. B.II.31). A frequent structuring criterion is the performance principle, i. e. points at which the same activities are performed are amalgamated into organizational units. According to the size of the enterprise, this structuring can be graduated to different extents. Typical concepts for the individual levels are principal department, department and group.

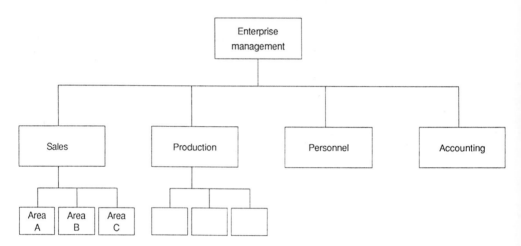

Fig. B.II.31: Hierarchy - organizational chart

In addition to this breakdown, other breakdowns according to planning levels can be formed to regulate planning and decision responsibilities. Such a structure is represented in Fig. B.II.32. It shows planning levels for an enterprise that are formed for the market and the production directions. Depending on the size of the organizational unit further sub-divisions can exist within these levels.

Whereas organizational charts generally display tree structures, planning relationships between areas can also display network structures. For instance, factories or branches can be responsible for several product areas.

Organizational units can exist over long periods or they can be formed for a limited time for certain projects.

The central object term in the organization description is the entity type ORGANIZATIONAL UNIT (see Fig. B.II.33). Organizational units can be distributed over several locations. Hierarchical superiority or subordination is expressed by the relationship type ORGANIZATION STRUCTURE. This reflects the perspective of the

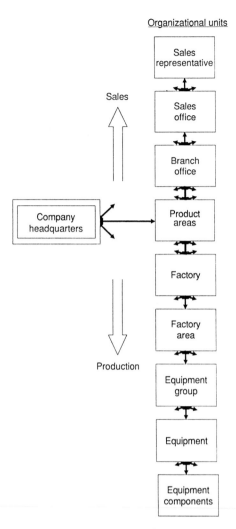

Fig. B.II.32: Planning levels

see *Scheer, CIM 1991, p. 128*

organigram in Fig. B.II.31, whereby a tree structure is assumed. The planning breakdown into function levels is expressed by the relationship type PLANNING STRUCTURE. Here, a network structure is represented.

The exchange of messages between organizational units which do not affect the database is also expressed by an n:m relationship within the entity type ORGANIZATIONAL UNIT. A typical application example of this is electronic mail.

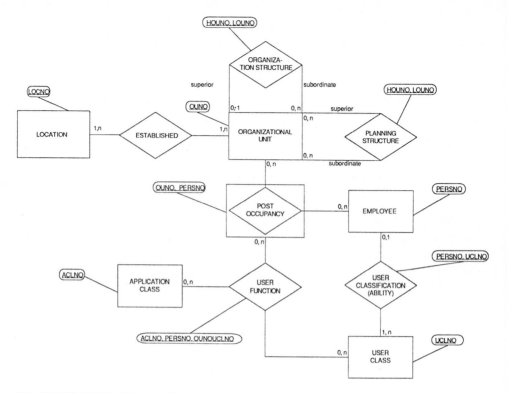

Fig. B.II.33: ERM of the requirements definition for organization view

### B.II.2.1.2 User Classes

The characteristics of a user of the information system are not determined by his membership of the organization, but by his individual abilities.

Users are represented by the entity type EMPLOYEE, and are identified by the personnel number PERSNO. Here, there is an overlap with the representation of the personnel management applications area, in which entity types for employees are also defined.

Consequently, only those factors are of interest here which relate to the development or use of information systems, and not the more strictly defined personnel management matters (wage and salary accounting, personnel utilization planning).

The overlap results from the fact that an information model itself represents an applications area, and the meta-information model is also an application description which has links with other applications.

Employees are assigned to organizational units by way of the relationship type POST OCCUPANCY. In this process an employee is always assigned directly, that is, to the hierarchically lowest level. Via the relationship type ORGANIZATION STRUCTURE all indirect superior and subordinate relationships can be derived. Since an employee can occupy several posts, e. g. when a departmental manager is commissioned to take over the management of another department in addition to his own, a maximum cardinality of n is applied from the view of the entity type EMPLOYEE. Since a post can also be occupied by several employees (job sharing) the same applies from the view of the ORGANIZATIONAL UNIT. A cardinality of 0 is applied as the lower limit in each case.

The aim here is not to construct all the relevant relationships of a personnel information system, this is rather the task of the personnel management or organization applications areas. Instead, the emphasis here is on the consideration of the employee as user of an EDP system. Nevertheless, care should be taken to ensure consistency between the terms used from the meta-view and the application view.

According to their knowledge and the frequency with which they use the EDP system, users are classified as
- occasional users,
- intensive users,
- experts
(see *Martin, Application Development 1982, p. 102 - 106; Davis/Olson, Management Information Systems 1984, p. 503 - 533*).
The entity type USER CLASS is introduced to describe this user classification. Each employee, insofar as he is a computer user, is assigned to one class.
The entity type APPLICATION CLASS is introduced to characterize different applications. It expresses general activities that a user can carry out with EDP support. Examples of application classes are independent data recording tasks, specialist processing using an interactive system, or electronic word processing.

The combination of EMPLOYEE, his assignment to an ORGANIZATIONAL UNIT (post occupancy), an APPLICATION CLASS and a USER CLASS thus allows a differentiated description of the use of EDP from the view of the requirements of the post, the capabilities of the employee and the relevant application class of the computer support. This relationship type is referred to as USER FUNCTION.
The user model developed can be extended to cover further characteristics, e. g. help functions or ergonomic requirements assigned to a user. The model presented is adequate for all subsequent discussions, however.

### B.II.2.1.3 The Organization Model

The information model of the requirements definition "organization view" has already been summarized in Fig. B.II.33.

### B.II.2.2 Procedural Model for Organization Modelling

Given the more restricted representational possibilities, the organization modelling has not been treated as extensively as the function modelling, so that the procedural model is

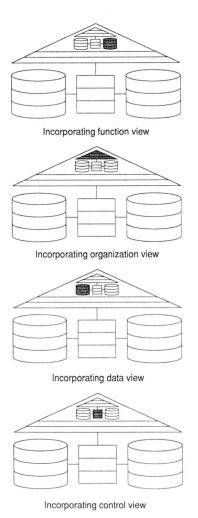

Incorporating function view

Incorporating organization view

Incorporating data view

Incorporating control view

Fig. B.II.34: Incorporation of the views of the procedural model for organization modelling

correspondingly simpler. For reasons of systematic uniformity, the section headings which were introduced for function modelling will be retained. The individual sections are incorporated in Fig. B.II.34.

### B.II.2.2.1 Function View

The essential function of organization modelling is the development of the user catalogue. Depending on the degree of detail, classification characteristics must be established and recorded for each application class and each user. The computer-technical transformation and implementation provides computerized support for the user catalogue associated with database systems (data dictionary) and user-friendly operating systems.

### B.II.2.2.2 Organization View

Organizational questions are primarily concerned with establishing the responsibility for classifying users. Here, self-assessment by the user, definition on the basis of post descriptions, interview techniques or tests can be employed.

### B.II.2.2.3 Data View

The data model of the procedural model in which the results of the organization modelling will be incorporated, is essentially identical to the information model of the organization description and has thus already been represented in Fig. B.II.33.

### B.II.2.2.4 Control View

There are no special features over and above those of the corresponding discussion of the function modelling.

### B.II.3 Requirements Definition of the Data View

The requirements definition of the data view is, along with the semantic data model, one of the most important building blocks of an information system. On the basis of the ARIS architecture, start and end events of a process chain are described in the semantic data model. At the same time, the descriptions of the relevant environmental conditions are also recorded. Fig. B.II.35 incorporates the data modelling block in the information system architecture. This block is shaded, the blocks already considered are dotted.

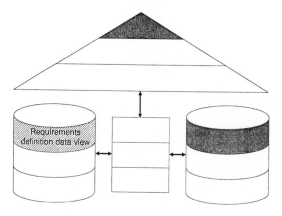

Fig. B.II.35: Incorporation of the requirements definition data view in ARIS

### B.II.3.1 Data Description

The data structure of an application area can be represented with the help of an ERM. The elements of this representation are at this stage also represented as an ERM. This is shown first for the simple ERM. It is then extended by some representational operators.

Since the model and the meta-model use the same terms (entity type, relationship type, etc.) the description involves verbal difficulties. In order to avoid misunderstandings, the suffix "requirements definition level" is used if the terms refer to the representation of applications within the information system. For additional clarity, the abbreviated relationships ETYP and RTYP are used for entity and relationship types at the requirements definition level, whereas the terms at the meta-level are written in full.

The simple ERM for structuring data from the applications consists of entity and relationship types which are linked together by edges. The extended ERM has in addition more exact specification of cardinalities, operators for specialization and generalization, reinterpretation of relationship types into entity types, etc.

At the meta-level, operators of the extended ERM are also used in the simple ERM.

**B.II.3.1.1 The Simple ERM**

The excerpt from a sales data structure shown in Fig. B.II.36 provides the starting point for the discussion.

CUSTOMER, ARTICLE and TIME are entity types which are linked together by the relationship types PURCHASE and ORDER. The order is identifiable as an event by its link with the entity type TIME, whereas the other elements represent conditions.

The elements are each assigned key attributes and descriptive attributes. Key attributes are underlined. The number of permitted instances of a relationship type from the perspective of an entity type is indicated by the limits 1, m, or n.

Fig. B.II.37 introduces the entity types ETYP and RTYP for the terms entity and relationship type at the requirements definition level. Instances thereof in the example are the entity types CUSTOMER, TIME and ARTICLE and the relationship types PURCHASE and ORDER. The instances are each identified by the key ETNO and RTNO.

Since the instances of different entity types can overlap (e. g. between CUSTOMER and SUPPLIER) Olle (see *Olle/Hagelstein/MacDonald, Information Systems 1988, p. 61*) introduced the relationship type "OVERLAP" between the entity type ETYP. This principle can also be applied to other elements (e. g. domains). Another possible refinement would be to distinguish between the elements and their names.

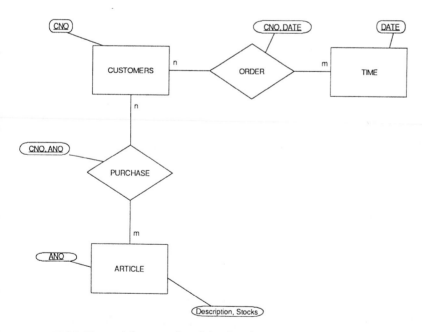

Fig. B.II.36: Excerpt from a sales data structure

The link between an entity type and a relationship type is generated at the requirements definition level by an edge. This is handled at the meta-level by introducing the relationship type EDGE in Fig. B.II.37. Attributes of the entity type EDGE are the number of permitted instances of the directional relationship. Since at the requirements definition level several edges lead from an entity type and several edges lead to a relationship type, limits of (1,n) in the (min.-max.) notation are set in each case.

At the requirements definition level several edges of diverse meanings can exist between an entity type and a relationship type (e. g. edges representing higher and lower level parts in the representation of the bill of materials structure). The entity type EDGE ROLE with the key ERNO is therefore introduced, in order to allow unambiguous identification of an edge. A specific edge is thus identified by the attribute combination ETNO, RTNO and ERNO.

Each entity type at the requirements definition level is assigned an identifying key attribute. They form the entity type KEY ATTRIBUTES. A 1:1 relationship exists between the entity type ETYP and the entity type KEY ATTRIBUTES. The upper and lower limits are therefore both 1. For example, the entity type customer CUSTOMER is assigned the unambiguous identifying key attribute CNO, and the entity type ARTICLE the article number ANO.

Relationship types are identified by the key attributes of the entity types with which they are linked. For this reason, there is no need to introduce a relationship between the entity type RTYP and KEY ATTRIBUTE. The key attributes are instead implicitly assigned via the EDGE relationship and the relationship between KEY ATTRIBUTE and ETYP. However, for easier understanding a (redundant) KEY ASSIGNMENT RTYP is introduced as an n:m relationship.

The entity types ETYP and RTYP are both attribute carriers at the requirements definition level, i. e. key attributes and other descriptive attributes are assigned to them at the requirements definition level. Therefore, they are both generalized to the entity type INFORMATION OBJECT.

Within an enterprise, data models can be constructed for specific applications areas such as marketing or production. The information objects (that is, entity and relationship types at the requirements definition level) which belong to such an area model are recorded via the entity type AREA MODEL and an n:m assignment to INFORMATION OBJECT.

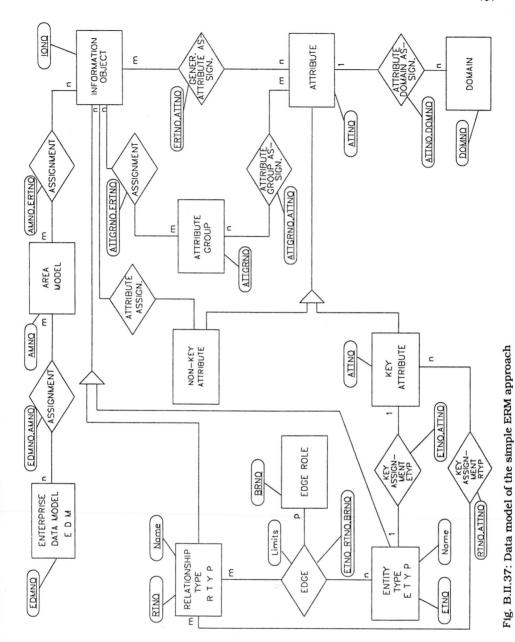

Fig. B.II.37: Data model of the simple ERM approach

The amalgamation of the area models then constitutes the entire enterprise data model (EDM) with the key EDMNO. Since there may be several versions of the area models and the enterprise data model, an n:m relationship applies between the entity type EDM and the entity type AREA MODEL. The version number is a component of the data model number, i. e. a new version number generates a new EDMNO or AMNO.

Once the entity and relationship types with their key attributes have been designed, in the second step the non-key attributes are determined and assigned.

The entity type KEY ATTRIBUTE which has already been introduced is a specialization of the general entity type ATTRIBUTE with the key attribute ATTNO. It is specialized into the entity types KEY ATTRIBUTE and NON-KEY ATTRIBUTE.

The non-key attributes are assigned to the attribute carrier INFORMATION OBJECT via a (1,n):(0,n) relationship. This means that an information object can possess several non-key attributes, which is also normally the case. On the other hand it also means that an attribute can be assigned to several attribute carriers, e. g. the attribute "name" to both the information object "customer" and the information object "supplier".

The "GENERAL ATTRIBUTE ASSIGNMENT" between ATTRIBUTE and INFORMATION OBJECT includes (with redundancy) both key and non-key references. It is used to simplify the further development undertaken later.

Attributes which belong together in terms of their contents can be aggregated into a group. For example, the attribute group "address" includes the attributes "street name, house number, post code and town". It is possible to form overlapping attribute groups, so that a (1,n):(0,n) relationship between the entity type ATTRIBUTE and ATTRIBTUE GROUP exists. An attribute group must contain at least one attribute, whereas not every attribute must be assigned to an attribute group.

Information objects can also be linked directly with attribute groups.

The value set of an attribute is indicated by the entity type DOMAIN. Each attribute can be assigned one domain. For example, for the attribute "name" the domain can store all the names that arise in the form of a dictionary, and for numerical values the numerical range can be defined.

The (1,n):(1,n) relationship between ATTRIBUTE and INFORMATION OBJECT allows a largely non-redundant management of the attributes and the domains. The term ATTRIBUTE thus includes here the smallest organizational unit in the semantic structuring of information. The term data element is also frequently used for this (see *Ortner/Rössner/Söllner, Entwicklung und Verwaltung standardisierter Datenelemente 1980, p. 19*). If the term data element is introduced as an independent unit of information then the assignment of a data element to an information object is referred to as an ATTRIBUTE. The previously coined term ATTRIBUTE is then replaced by the term DATA ELEMENT, and the "GENERAL ATTRIBUTE ASSIGNMENT" is replaced by the term "ATTRIBUTE". Fig. B.II.38 contrasts the two representational methods. However, both representations are identical in terms of their contents. Consequently, in Fig. B.II.37 the suffix "DATA ELEMENT" is added in brackets.

This completes the development of the information model for the simple ERM approach.

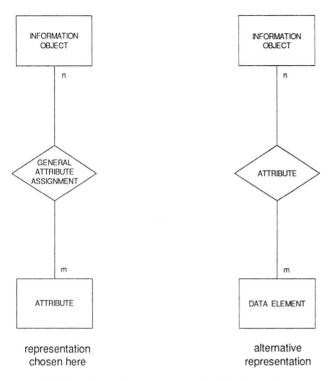

representation
chosen here

alternative
representation

Fig. B.II.38: Alternative representation for data elements

**B.II.3.1.2 The Extended ERM**

In contrast with the simple ERM approach, the following extensions are introduced (see Fig. B.II.39):

- reinterpretation of relationship types as entity types,
- application of the specialization/generalization operation,
- formation of complex objects from entity and relationship types.

The more exact specification of cardinalities by the declaration of upper and lower limits is simply expressed by the attribution of the relationship type EDGE and leads to no other changes in the information model.

The possibility of reinterpreting a relationship type as an entity type requires that, at the meta-level of Fig. B.II.40, specialized entity types for the original and the reinterpreted entity types be introduced alongside the general entity type ETYP. A reinterpreted entity type, therefore, appears twice: it is first an element of the general entity type ETYP or the specialization RETYP and at the same time it is a specialization of RTYP.

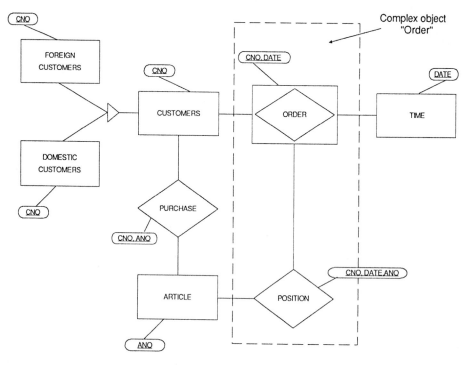

Fig. B.II.39: Extended ERM representation

Since edges run from both the elementary entity types and the reinterpreted entity types to the relationship types, the relationship type EDGE is formed between the general entity type ETYP and RTYP.

The introduction of the specialization/generalization operation at the requirements definition level gives rise to the formation of the GENERALIZATION or SPECIALIZATION VIEW: For example, the breakdown of the entity type CUSTOMERS at the requirements definition level into FOREIGN CUSTOMERS and DOMESTIC CUSTOMERS presents the view "market region". "Market region" is therefore an instance of the entity type SPECIALIZATION VIEW. At the application level, one view leads to several entity types (FOREIGN and DOMESTIC CUSTOMERS), whereas in the reverse direction an entity type should belong unequivocally to only one specialization view.

Since specialization involves taking over the key attributes of the higher level entity type, this means that one key concept now applies to several entity types (e. g. the customer number for the general entity type CUSTOMERS and also for the specialization DOMESTIC and FOREIGN CUSTOMERS).

Consequently, the cardinality between KEY ASSIGNMENT and the original entity type OETYP is of type (1,1).

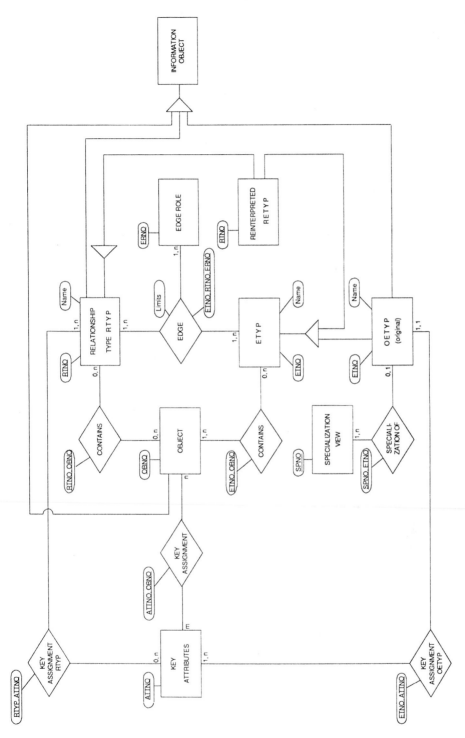

Fig. B.II.40: ERM for the requirements definition of the data view

The key attributes for the relationship types can be formed via the edge assignment from the keys of the entity types involved. For clarity of representation, however, a special relationship type KEY ASSIGNMENT is formed.

If a relationship type is reinterpreted, the new entity type takes over the key attributes of the original relationship type.

An ERM breaks down a complex situation into a lucid structure. However, as a result, the relation to the overall situation does not always remain immediately obvious. For this reason, the term "COMPLEX OBJECT" is introduced, which amalgamates several entity and relationship types which belong to one object of interest (see *Dittrich, Stand und Tendenzen der "nachrelationalen" Datenbanktechnologie 1990*; see also *Härder, Grenzen und Erweiterungsmöglichkeiten relationaler Datenbanksysteme 1989*).

A complex object consists of several entity and relationship types. An example is a drawing which contains the entire geometric structure of an assembly and which is composed of several entity and relationship types (FORMS, SURFACES, EDGES, POINTS, etc.), or a contract containing a complex data structure. An order with its items can also be regarded as a complex object (see Fig. B.II.39). The individual objects at the application level (e. g. DRAWING, CONTRACT, ORDER, ...) are then instances of the entity type OBJECT at the meta-level. Since objects can also overlap, the cardinalities are always set at (0,n) or (1,n). The relationship between an object and its components can be characterized by an "is part of" relationship.

The entity types OETYP, RTYP and OBJECT are thus the carriers of the descriptive attributes and hence information objects.
The attributes of RETYP correspond to those of the original entity type RTYP. They are, therefore, not re-assigned.

The link with attribute assignment, which is carried out in the second step of the data model design, is executed in the extended form in the same way as was already discussed for the simplified ERM representation.

### B.II.3.2 Procedural Model for Data Modelling

The incorporation of the views of the procedural model is shown in Fig. B.II.41.

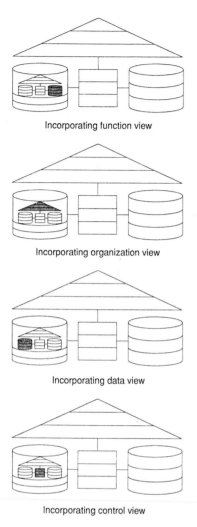

Incorporating function view

Incorporating organization view

Incorporating data view

Incorporating control view

Fig. B.II.41: Incorporation of the views of the procedural model for data modelling

### B.II.3.2.1 Function View

The specification of the area data models through to the enterprise-wide data model is a considerable undertaking. The procedural sequence is represented in rough form in Fig. B.II.42. The individual procedures can be broken down further, and loops to preceding procedures are also possible.

The computer support covers above all the use of graphics tools for creating the entity-relationship diagram. In the context of the design specification, it is necessary to carry out adjustments of the conceptual design to the EDP implementation, depending on the tool used. Not all tools offer methods supporting the generalization/specialization operators used here, or the transformation of relationship types into entity types. Many tools are also based on the Bachman diagram methodology, which only permits a coarser semantic treatment (in Bachman diagrams, for instance, all relationship types which are attribute carriers are represented as entity types). An impression of the range of graphical representation is given in Fig. B.II.43. Fig. B.II.44 presents an example of tool-supported ERM representation with the help of the widely used IEW system.

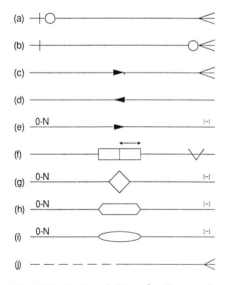

Fig. B.II.42: Function model for data modelling

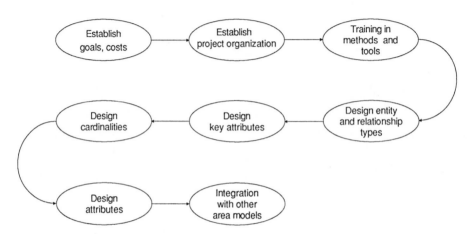

Fig. B.II.43: Possibilities for the graphical representation of relationships with cardinalities

from: *Olle/Hagelstein/MacDonald, Information Systems 1988, p. 198*

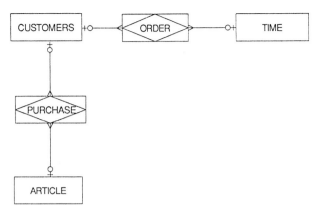

Fig. B.II.44: ERM representation in IEW

Computer support can also be provided in the testing of integrity conditions. This applies, for example, to the integration of area models into a comprehensive enterprise-wide data model. Consistency or inconsistency of terms used must be checked. The same also applies if the creation of the single enterprise-wide model has been generated using both top-down and bottom-up approaches. Here too, the information objects that have been established on different routes must be checked for terminological consistency.

In addition, unwanted cycles in the data model can be exposed and redundant parts of the data model recognized.

However, the validation of the data model using tools is only possible within limits. Fundamentally, design of a data structure is an intellectual process, which is not completely submissible to automated rules.

Using prototyping support in the creation of the data model, however, can allow the early detection of inconsistencies and lack of conformity with user requirements. For a more detailed description of a procedural model for data modelling and the use of tools see *Scheer, Enterprise-Wide Data Modelling 1990.*

Computerized data model design allows a multiplicity of evaluations of information objects according to their descriptive components, or the extraction of related data structures from a global model.

### B.II.3.2.2 Organization View

In the organization view the question of the organizational units involved in the creation of a data model occupies the foreground. As well as employees concerned with information management, the top management of the firm also needs to be involved in specifying the strategic goals of a data model. In the subsequent execution of the project it is necessary, just as in the function modelling, to establish a project organization which is both temporally and financially controlled by concrete milestone deadlines.

In terms of computer support, both the administration of the project management and the networking of those involved in the creation of a data model are required.

### B.II.3.2.3 Data View

The data view concerns the management of the meta-data model. The EDP concept must take into account the conditions for using tools for creating the ERM. This applies especially with respect to the types of information objects to be adopted and defined, as well as the possibilities for supporting design operators. Furthermore, the data view of the meta-model relates to the management of the defined information objects and to the integrity checks that need to be carried out.

### B.II.3.2.4 Control View

The procedural model covers both the functional process of creating a data model and the organization view, i. e. the assignment of those responsible for the individual procedures, as well as the result of the data view. By the assignment of organizational units, functions, and data models, differentiated documentation can be provided for the various versions (see Fig. B.II.29).

Thus, it is necessary within the context of the control view to settle the responsibility of organizational units for the contents of the repository. The database administrator, that is the organizational unit responsible for data management, cannot take over responsibility for checking the contents of the data model. In addition, it is necessary to establish the specialist responsibility not only for the creation but also for the current operation.

### B.II.4  Requirements Definition of the Control View

The task of the control modelling is to reunite the separately considered views (function, organization, and data). In addition, dynamic aspects of the information architecture are considered, since the linking up of the views allows the description of changes of state and hence the dynamic behaviour of the system.

First, pairwise relationships between the architectural blocks are considered, and then all three views are linked together.

The incorporation of this block is shown in Fig.B.II.45.

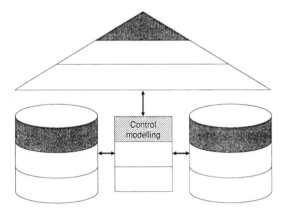

Fig. B.II.45: Incorporation of the control modelling in ARIS

#### B.II.4.1  Description of the Control View

#### B.II.4.1.1  Linking Functions and Organization

The link between function and organizational units can be represented at various levels of detail.

In a function level model the main functions of a process chain are allocated to the organizational units responsible. Fig. B.II.46 illustrates this for the planning level structure introduced in Fig. B.II.32 for an industrial firm with logistic chain, product development, master data management and controlling functions.

Fig. B.II.47 shows the function assignment in a commonly used matrix representation. The example shows an excerpt from a practical case of order processing in the industrial goods industry. The entire order processing consists in this particular case of about 150

112

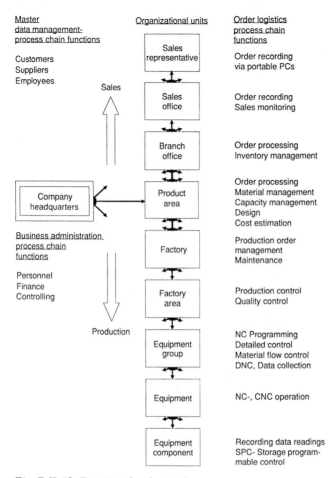

Master
data management-
process chain functions

Customers
Suppliers
Employees

Sales

Company
headquarters

Business administration
process chain
functions

Personnel
Finance
Controlling

Production

Organizational units

Sales
representative

Sales
office

Branch
office

Product
area

Factory

Factory
area

Equipment
group

Equipment

Equipment
component

Order logistics
process chain
functions

Order recording
via portable PCs

Order recording
Sales monitoring

Order processing
Inventory management

Order processing
Material management
Capacity management
Design
Cost estimation

Production order
management
Maintenance

Production control
Quality control

NC Programming
Detailed control
Material flow control
DNC, Data collection

NC-, CNC operation

Recording data readings
SPC- Storage program-
mable control

Fig. B.II.46: Function level model

functions. A distinction has not yet been drawn between computerized and manual processes.

Insofar as several organizational units are involved in one function, the extent of the involvement can be described more closely by declarations such as "responsible", "actively involved" or "associated". A further concrete example is given by J. Martin (see *Martin, Information Engineering, Planning and Analysis 1990, p. 58 f.*).

The function level model, or the matrix representation of function assignment, is represented in the information model by the relationship type FUNCTION ASSIGNMENT (see Fig. B.II.48). The assignment is restricted here to the main functions.

By linking the functions with the associated processes, all organizational units that are involved in a business process can be determined. Conversely, from the viewpoint of the

| Functions \ Organizational units | Company management | Marketing | Co.planning & organization | Branch management | Personnel | Cost account. & Controlling | Sales | Distribution | R & D | Production | Purchasing | Material administration |
|---|---|---|---|---|---|---|---|---|---|---|---|---|
| Market analysis | i | r | x | x | | | i | | | | | |
| Prodn. program planning | r | i | i | x | x | x | i | | x | x | x | |
| Offer processing | | | | | | | r | | | | | |
| Order management | | | | | | | r | | | | | |
| Product development | i | | | x | x | i | i | | r | i | i | |
| Production planning | | | i | | i | x | i | | i | r | i | x |
| Material purchasing | | | | | | | | | | | r | i |
| Inventory management | | | | | | | | x | | | | r |
| Prodn. control and monitoring | | | | | | x | x | | | r | | |
| Quality assurance | | | | x | | | x | x | i | r | i | r |
| Dispatch | | | | i | | | i | r | | | | |
| Cost accounting and monitoring | x | | x | i | x | r | | | x | x | x | |
| Finance & investment planning | i | | r | x | x | i | | | | x | x | |
| Personnel planning and development | i | | i | x | r | x | | | | x | x | |
| Stock-taking & annual settlement | i | | x | i | | r | | | | x | x | |

r = responsible    i = actively involved    x = associated

Fig. B.II.47: Matrix representation of function assignment

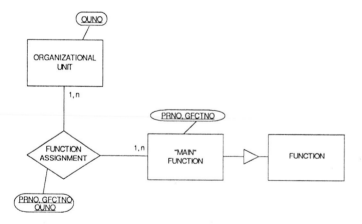

Fig. B.II.48: ERM for function assignment

organizational unit, all the functions in which it is involved can be determined along with the process chains to which they belong.

As regards the cardinalities, it is assumed on the one hand that any organizational unit is involved in at least one function and that a function is assigned to at least one organizational unit. On the other hand the cardinality "n" indicates that a function can be processed by several organizational units, and thus the distribution of a function to several planning levels within a process chain is possible.

This definition represents the creation of a hierarchy for a process chain, i. e., identical functions, such as "availability check" can be carried out with various planning timescales and reference objects (order, operation) at various levels (factory, factory area, machine group, etc.).

At a more detailed level not only can main functions be assigned to the broad function levels of an enterprise, but also detailed user transactions to the organizational posts or even specific users (see Fig. B.II.49). To this end, the term "user transaction" which was introduced in the function modelling is adopted. It is linked with the term "post occupancy" which was created for the organization modelling. In this way, a specific user can be allowed access to defined user transactions in the context of his post. A user transaction can thereby be executed from various posts and persons. A post can (but does not have to) be authorized for several user transactions, so that a cardinality with the lower limit of 0 results.

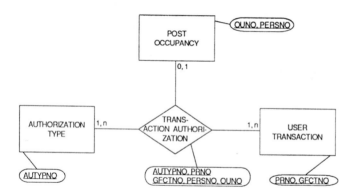

Fig. B.II.49: Assignment of transactions to specific users

### B.II.4.1.2 Linking Functions and Data

The link between data and functions is obvious, since a function can be described as the transformation of input data into output data.

For this reason, many methods which are actually thought of as function representations, also link the function and data views. Examples are the SADT method or DeMarco diagrams, which will be considered in more detail below.

### B.II.4.1.2.1 Event Control

Fig. B.II.50 presents the excerpt "customer request processing" from the "order processing" process chain. The customer request initiates the processing, whereby additional information about customers and articles are accessed. The result of the processing is the customer offer. In the course of processing, information about customers and articles (e. g. customer turnover and stocks on hand) can be altered.
Events therefore control the execution of the process both as the initiators and the results of functions.

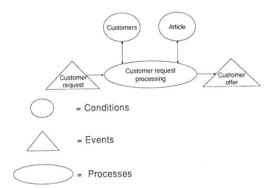

Fig. B.II.50: Process chain: customer request processing

In the ARIS approach both events and conditions of the relevant environment are represented in the form of data, i. e. by the general entity type INFORMATION OBJECT. To differentiate, this is then specialized into the two entity types EVENT and CONDITION (see Fig. B.II.51). At the requirements definition level events are formed as relationship types which are linked with the entity type TIME.
The fact that events initiate functions and are also the result of functions is expressed by the relationship types INITIATION and RESULT. A function can be initiated by one or more events. At the same time a function can also have several events as its result. An event can also be the result of several functions, e. g. the completion of a project by the completion of several parallel functions. This connection between functions and events also applies within a function if it is broken down into sub-functions. With a coarser function breakdown, such as is shown in the examples used, "intermediate" results are

116

recorded in the database as status changes in the environment, without them initiating new functions.

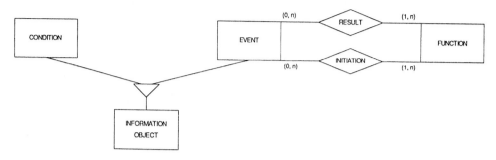

Fig. B.II.51: Event Control

### B.II.4.1.2.2 Data Flow

In addition to event control, which is effected at the information object level, a data flow can also be specified in more detail using attributes. Fig. B.II.52 describes customer request processing as a DeMarco data flow diagram. The information objects (events and conditions) are represented within double lines. The essential attributes needed by the functions are assigned to the arrows. This approach has been extended by Ward and Mellor to real-time systems (see *Ward/Mellor, Structured Development for Real-Time Systems 1985*).

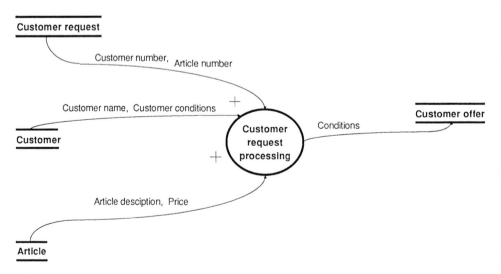

Fig. B.II.52: DeMarco data flow diagram for customer request processing

The data flow is represented by the relationship OPERATION between FUNCTION and ATTRIBUTE ASSIGNMENT of the meta-model (see Fig. B.II.53). The relationship

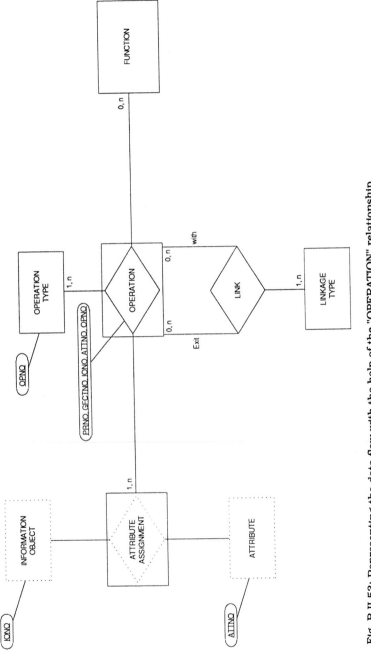

Fig. B.II.53: Representing the data flow with the help of the "OPERATION" relationship

OPERATION also makes it possible to represent the operations that can be carried out on attributes by a function in greater detail. These individual operations are:

- create a data element,
- delete a data element,
- update a data element,
- read only a data element.

ENTITY TYPE

Key
C: Create
R: Read Only
U: Update
D: Delete

| PROCESS | Employee (1) | Contract Employee (2) | Applicant (3) | HR Compensation Regs, Plans, etc. (4) | HR Benefits Regs & Plans (5) | HR Staffing Requirements & Plans (6) | Job Requisition (7) | Stockholder (8) | Boardmember (9) | Misc. Contacts/VIPs (10) | Financial Plans (11) | Accounting Regs, Practices (12) | Ledger Accounts (13) | Customer Purchase Order/Invoice (14) | Customer Payments (15) | Other Income (16) |
|---|---|---|---|---|---|---|---|---|---|---|---|---|---|---|---|---|
| 1 Evaluate Financial Proposals | | | | | | | | | | | | | | | | |
| 2 Estimate Near-Term Earnings | | | | | | | | | | | | | R | | | |
| 3 Budget Finances | R | R | | R | R | | | | | | CRUD | R | CRUD | | | |
| 4 Receive Funds | | | | | | | | | | | | R | | R | CRUD | CRUD |
| 5 Pay Funds | R | | | | | | | | | | | R | | | | |
| 6 Report Finances | R | | | | | | | | | | | R | RU | R | R | R |
| 7 Administer Taxes | | | | | | | | | | | | R | R | | R | R |
| 8 Maintain Financial Reg, Policies | | | | | | | | | | | R | CRUD | | | | |
| 9 Audit Finances | | | | | | | | | | | | R | R | | R | R |
| 10 Manage Financial Investments | | | | | | | | CRUD | | | | R | | | | |
| 11 Plan Humane Resources | R | R | | | CRUD | CRUD | | | R | | R | | | | | |
| 12 Acquire Personnel | CRUD | CRUD | CRUD | | | R | R | | CRU | | | | | | | |
| 13 Position People in Jobs | | R | | | | R | RU | | R | | | | | | | |
| 14 Terminate/Retire People | RUD | RUD | | | | | | | RUD | | | | | | | |
| 15 Plan Carreer Paths | RU | | | R | R | R | | | | | | | | | | |
| 16 Develop Skills/Motivation | RU | RU | | | R | R | | | | | | | | | | |
| 17 Manage Individual Emp Relations | RU | RU | | | R | | | | | | | | | | | |
| 18 Manage Benefits Programs | | | | | CRUD | | | | | | | | | | | |
| 19 Comply with Govt HR Regulations | R | | | | R | | | | | | | | | | | |
| 20 Maintain HR Regs, Policies | | | | CRUD | | CRUD | | | | | | | | | | |
| 21 Determine Production Requirement | | | | | | | | | | | | | | R | | |
| 22 Schedule Production | R | R | | | | | | | | | | | | | | |

Fig. B.II.54: Process-entity type-matrix

from: Martin, Information Engineering, Planning and Analysis 1990, p. 272

Here, it is useful to establish in all cases the highest operation level for a data element. These assignments are often defined in tabular form (see Fig. B.II.54, from: *Martin, Information Engineering, Planning and Analysis 1990, p. 272*, see also the clustering method on p. 175).

The deletion of an entity at the requirements definition level can be interpreted as the deletion of the key attributes of the entity, and the creation of an entity as the creation of the key attributes. Thus, the relationship type OPERATION represents all the possible manipulations which carry out functions on their information objects or attributes. The entity type OPERATION TYPE is formed for the individual kinds of operation, so that OPERATION is the link between OPERATION TYPE, FUNCTION, and ATTRIBUTE ASSIGNMENT.

The operations carried out by a function can be linked together logically, as has already been indicated in the DeMarco diagram. For example, several data fields may be required for one function, so that for the read function an "and"-link exists between them. These linkage possibilities are represented by the relationship type LINKAGE between the operations. The kind of link is shown by the entity type LINKAGE TYPE (Boolean operations are possible here, for example). It should be noted, however, that the constructs introduced do not allow all possible logical links between diverse incoming and outgoing data elements to be created.

The links between FUNCTION and ATTRIBUTE ASSIGNMENT represented by the term OPERATION support both a more data-oriented and a more function-oriented view. This means, that both data- and function-oriented representations can be generated from the meta-model of Fig. B.II.53. Specific methods often contain both views. For instance, the SADT method (Structured Analysis Design Technique) expresses both perspectives in the terms activity box and data box (see Fig. B.II.55).

The activity box generates the relationships with the incoming, controlling and outgoing data, whereby the processor describes the transformation rules, that is, the operations employed.

The data box considers which functions an information object and its attributes generate, and in which further functions it is used.

As a result of the strict separation of data and functions no direct data exchange between functions occurs in the ARIS architecture, instead, this always occurs via the database. For this reason, the result of the customer request processing in Fig. B.II.52, the customer offer, is not passed on directly to the next processing function, but leads to an

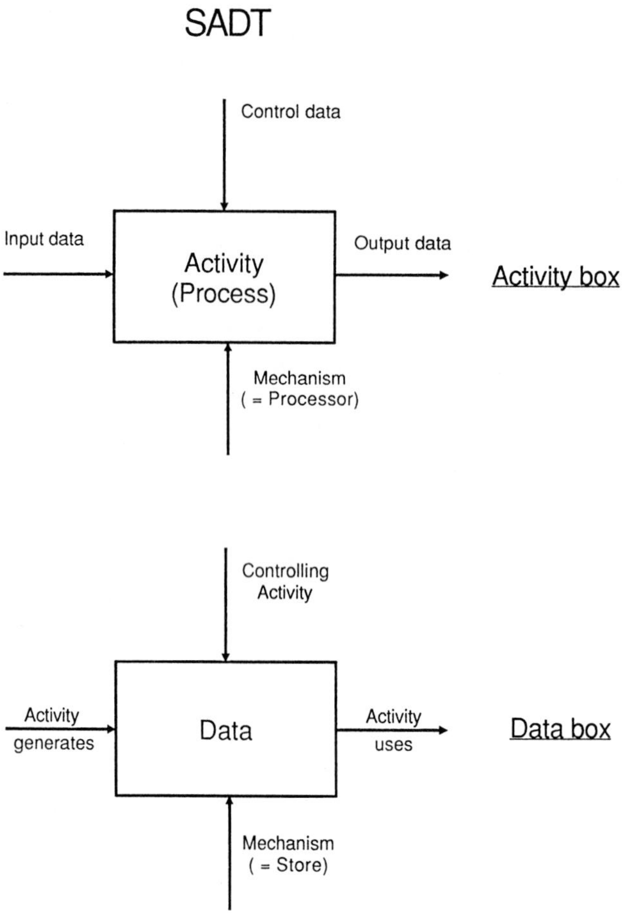

# SADT

Control data

Input data

**Activity
(Process)**

Output data

**Activity box**

Mechanism
( = Processor)

Controlling
Activity

Activity
generates

**Data**

Activity
uses

**Data box**

Mechanism
( = Store)

Fig. B.II.55: Activity and data view of the SADT method

alteration in the database, that is, the creation of the information object customer offer. This is then an event which initiates new processing functions.

The event control of functional processes finds its equivalent in the trigger control of the design specification. This term is also used at the requirements definition level to increase the descriptive continuity, so that reference can then be made to it later. On initiation of a function, data are generally passed on for processing. This can be represented as a request for the necessary data by the function concerned via the "operation" following event initiation (see Fig. B.II.53). However, the direct connection can also be represented along the lines of Fig. B.II.56. Here, an event initiates a function. The initiation simultaneously transfers attributes to the function in the form of "trigger messages". These issues will be considered in more detail in the description of the EDP concept.

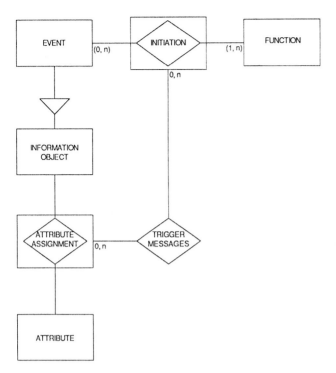

Fig. B.II.56: Explicit representation of trigger messages

### B.II.4.1.2.3 Object-Oriented Modelling

The breakdown of an application system into data and function views has been criticised in the context of the object-oriented approach. Examples of the use of the term object-oriented are found in connection with object-oriented programming languages or object-oriented specifications (see *Ferstl/Sinz, Objektmodellierung betrieblicher Informationssysteme 1990; Meyer, Object-oriented Software Construction 1988; Schreiber, Einsatz objektorientierter Konzepte 1990; Association for Computing Machinery (ACM) (eds), Objektorientierte Programmierung 1990*). These approaches always express a holistic viewpoint. Design based on views is objected to on the grounds that it destroys the natural coherence between functions and data. The data structures in an enterprise-wide data model cannot be checked regarding their completeness or accuracy without a function view. The reduction in redundancy that is achieved by the breakdown into views is certainly accepted, but not regarded as an adequate justification (see *Zimmermann, Einsatz objektorientierter Softwaretechnologie im Rechnungswesen 1990*).

In the context of object-oriented modelling the data are therefore combined with the functions (methods) to be carried out on them in order to generate an object description. Since all the functions which can be carried out on an object's data are assigned to the object, they form a data capsule.

The entire system, therefore, consists of objects; changes to the system are expressed by messages which the objects exchange with each other and which generate reactions. The difference between the view-oriented approach and the object space with defined objects (consisting of functions and data) and the messages which occur between them is shown in Fig. B.II.57. Since Zimmermann provides an object-oriented treatment of an easily comprehensible business application example from financial accounting, this will be used as a basis for the following discussion.

Identical objects are combined into object classes.

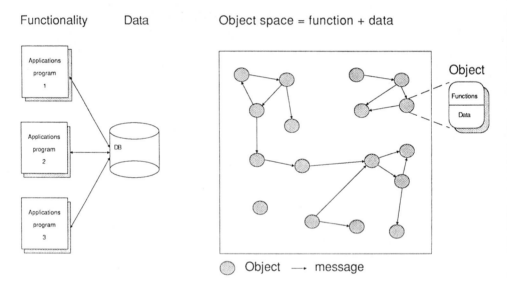

Fig. B.II.57: Traditional and object-oriented systems

from: *Zimmermann, Einsatz objektorientierter Softwaretechnologie im Rechnungswesen 1990, p. 239*

Fig. B.II.58 shows both the classes and the instances of the object ACCOUNT. The method "creation of a new account" is defined for the account class "account". This applies only to the creation of a new instance, that is a new account, and therefore relates to the class itself. These kinds of methods are referred to as constructors. Instance variables, or attributes, which are assigned values for each of the instances, are also specified.

This representation corresponds largely to the data type description in the entity-relationship model, in which both information objects and attributes are defined. In addition, methods are assigned to an object class, which can be carried out with the individual instances. Examples of such methods for accounts are bookings, balance calculations.

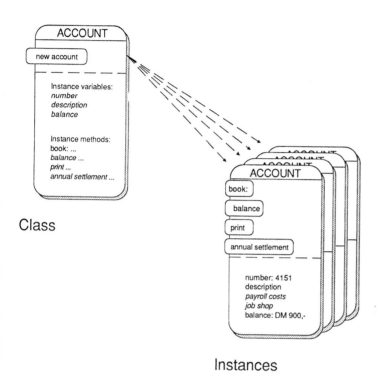

Class

Instances

Fig. B.II.58: The accounts class with its instances

from: *Zimmermann, Einsatz objektorientierter Softwaretechnologie im Rechnungswesen 1990, p. 242*

An essential property of object-oriented design is its emphasis on inheritance. In creating classes, lower level classes (sub-classes) always take on the definitions of variables and methods of the higher level classes. Of course, a sub-class can extend these, or overwrite the definition from the higher level class.

By the creation of sub-classes incremental changes to the system can be effected very simply and without redundancy. This is seen as a special advantage as compared with the so-called "classical" approaches, where small changes necessitate the copying and amendment of entire programs or program parts. This procedure is shown in Fig. B.II.59 for the account example introduced above. Alterations to the software system are

124

generated in the context of object-oriented programming by way of the exchange of messages. A message is always sent from one object class to another, and generally carries the name of the function to be carried out by the receiving object. For example, an object can send an account object a message of the type "book". This then initiates a booking function in the receiving account object. At the same time a parameter of the message passes on the value to be booked. A message is thus defined by sender (implicitly by way of the return value), recipient, message name and parameter.

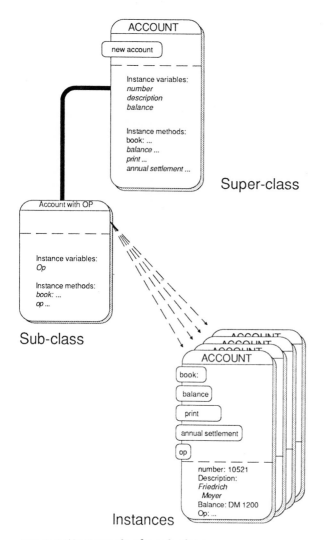

Fig. B.II.59: Example of a sub-class

from: *Zimmermann, Einsatz objektorientierter Softwaretechnologie im Rech-nungswesen 1990, p. 244*

However, the structural elements of the object-oriented modelling represented are not so far removed from modelling based on views as proponents of the object-oriented approach sometimes maintain. For example, the formation of classes and inheritance can be directly linked with the data modelling approach. Here, too, conceptual classes (entity types and relationship types) are defined. At the same time sub-classes are formed via the "is a" relationship. The inheritance of the higher level attributes (instance variables in the object-oriented programming sense) is also commonplace. For this reason, a similar formulation would have been developed in the entity-relationship model context for the bookkeeping example. Of course, the links with the functions and event control by way of messages would not have been generated.

The separation of data and functions is undertaken within the view-oriented design for reasons of simplicity, but not in order to emphasize the independence of the views. For this reason, the ARIS architecture reconstructs the link via the control view. Consequently, the information objects of a data model can at least provide suggestions for the creation of objects. Frequently, however, many objects are identical with the information objects. Since the methods and variables can also be linked with the terms data element (attribute) and functions, the object-oriented modelling can be interpreted as the linking of the function and data models. In the "semantic object-oriented modelling" (SOM) approach of Ferstl and Sinz this principle is taken further in a formal procedural concept (see *Ferstl/Sinz, Objektmodellierung betrieblicher Informationssysteme 1990*).

From the data view, which can be represented by a special formulation of the entity-relationship model (SERM = structured ERM), both class definitions and communication paths can be derived. The classes (object types) are concurrent with the entity types of the data model, and the relationship types indicate the communication paths (interaction channels) by way of the key relationships (see *Ferstl/Sinz, Objektmodellierung betrieblicher Informationssysteme 1990, p. 572*).

A procedural model creates process object types, which describe process chains and comprive the process chain-specific segment of the object types and their associated interactions.

The "process" object type controls the execution of process chains using appropriate messages.

The connections between an object-oriented and a view-oriented design are represented in the meta-model of Fig. B.II.60.

Fig. B.II.60 first shows in the middle the central term OBJECT CLASS, which represents the creation of sub-classes using the relationship type CLASS CREATION. A net structure within the term OBJECT CLASS is permitted. The term object class comprises both super-classes and sub-classes.

The instance variables defining an object class are assigned to it via a relationship with the entity type DATA ELEMENTS. In this way, the relationship with data modelling is obvious.

The methods belonging to an object class are assigned to it via the relationship type METHODS, which points to the functions. The reference to the function model is created here.

It is important that the relationship types INSTANCE VARIABLE  and METHODS possess a cardinality of (0,1) from the perspective of the relevant terms in the data and function model, that is, there is a maximum of **one** counterpart. This means first that each data element and each function, if they correspond in type and degree of detail to one instance variable or method, can be assigned directly, so that only a notational difference between the relationship types is generated.

At the same time the cardinality implies that a data element is managed by only one data class, and also that a function can only arise in one object class. This highlights the lack of redundancy in the object-oriented modelling.

In the inheritance of sub-classes the variables and functions taken over are not listed again in the sub-class, instead, they are automatically accessible via the class creation process. Only the additional or superimposed data and functions are assigned.

The formation of object classes is a similarly creative process to that of the formation of information objects. It requires the same level of applications knowledge and methodological understanding.

The information objects of a data model are frequently identical with the objects of an object-oriented design. The close correspondence between entity types and object types, which Ferstl and Sinz undertake, is not followed here, since in principle each information object (i. e. each relationship type) can come in question as an object type.

Messages first generate a link between OBJECT CLASS by the specification of the sender and the recipient(s), the function (method) to be executed by the recipient, and the parameters transferred for controlling the function.

A method (function) can send messages to other objects while processing an object. This link is generated by incorporating the initiating method in the message definition.

A message is thus characterized by the key attributes of:
- sender (object),
- recipient (object),
- initiating method,
- control method, and
- parameter.

The reference to the functional procedures in the form of process chains is generated by the link from the entity type FUNCTIONS to PROCESS, which was established in the function model context.

If selected functions, e. g. processes as start elements of process chains, should also possess object characteristics, that is, be capable of carrying out methods and sending messages, this can be achieved by an assignment between the entity types PROCESS and OBJECT CLASS.

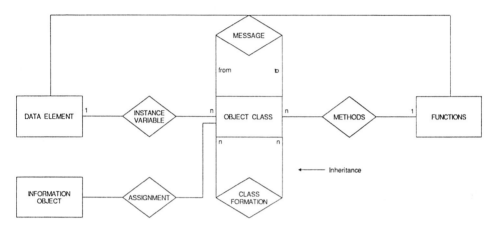

Fig. B.II.60: Object-oriented design

### B.II.4.1.3 Linking Organization and Data

As with the link between data and functions, the relationships between organization and data can be described at various levels of detail. Analogous to the function level model, in which broad functions, described as main functions, are assigned to the planning levels of an enterprise, this can also be carried out for data (see the data level model in Fig. B.II.61).

The link can also be established in tabular form, whereby the data linkages can be established more precisely by entries such as "generally responsible", "authorized" or "responsible for updates".

Fig. B.II.62 shows the associated meta-model, in which the separation of the sub-entity type PLANNING LEVEL from the general entity type ORGANIZATIONAL UNIT makes the relatively broad level of detail obvious.

In a more detailed analysis authorizations can be defined at the operative level. The operations might relate to the "creation", "deletion" "updating" or "reading" of data

128

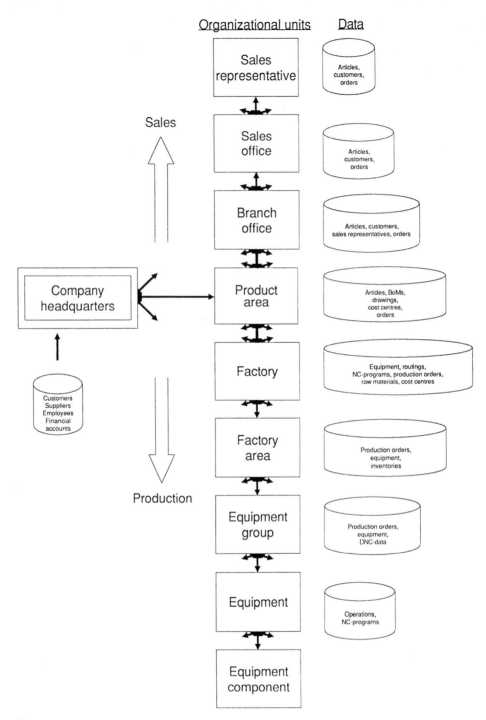

Fig. B.II.61: Data level model

elements. These kinds of authorization can in turn be represented in tabular form. The information model for this is shown in Fig. B.II.63. The user is defined by "post occupancy", i. e. by the assignment of an employee to a specific organizational unit.

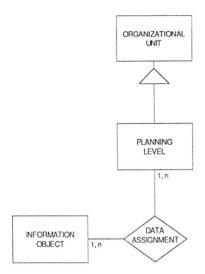

Fig. B.II.62: ERM linking organization and data

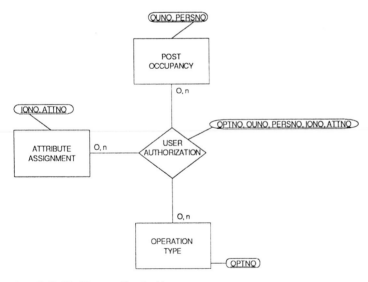

Fig. B.II.63: User authorizations

130

The "USER AUTHORIZATION" is thus defined at the attribute level. This means that the attributes which are allowed to be processed are established for each operation type and user. Additional limits concerning the value instances of an attribute can be established, e. g. that an employee in the personnel department is only allowed to read salaries up to a certain amount. This can then be specified more precisely by attribute values of the relationship type AUTHORIZATION. It is also conceivable that several operation types could be provided for a post assignment with various authorizations. For example, a personnel employee may be allowed to update values up to a certain salary limit, and to read values up to another salary limit.

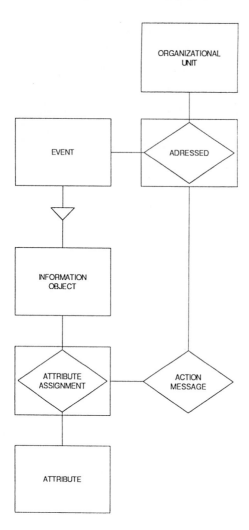

Fig. B.II.64: Event control of organizational units

Analogous to the event control of functions, organizational units can also be activated by events. In this context, one refers to action-oriented process control. Fig. B.II.64 represents, as a function trigger analogy, the initiation of activities by organizational units via the transfer of the relevant data elements in the form of action messages.

### B.II.4.1.4 Linking Functions, Organization and Data

This link combines all the components of the ARIS architecture. In a rougher approach this can be expressed by the process chain diagram already introduced (see Fig. B.I.02 above). In Fig. B.II.65 this is formulated as an information model. An element of the process chain diagram indicates the processing form (batch, online) in which a particular function is carried out by an organizational unit, and which information objects are thereby created, read or updated. Once again, it is established that the data are not transferred directly from one function to another, but that the transfer is always conducted via the data view.

Event control and communication relationships can also be represented with greater differentiation.

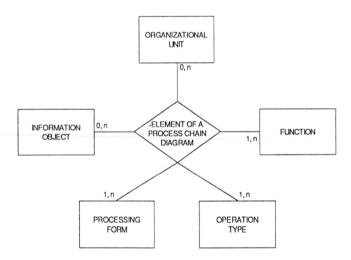

Fig. B.II.65: ERM of the process chain diagram

If events not only initiate EDP functions, but also occasion measures to be undertaken by specialist staff, then the organizational units are also affected by the event control.

In the definition of communication partners, the term external partner or external agent is used for the link with the outside world. Here, it is treated as a specialization of the term organizational unit, so that no new entity type is defined.

The most differentiated link can be generated by a relationship between the USER FUNCTION of the organization model and the OPERATION of the data-function assignment. This allows trigger and action messages to be exchanged in differentiated form, causes the initiation of functions, and generates the detailed assignment of users in the context of application functions defined for them.

The design method supported by Petri nets is also especially powerful. Although its practical implementation is not yet widespread, this method is very well suited to the modelling of office applications and process control. The special properties of Petri nets are that a problem can initially be described in very rough form in a static representation, and then continually refined until a model capable of handling simulations is generated. Particular characteristics of this are the transition from a static to a dynamic model, the representation of parallel processes and the incorporation of decisions and stochastic branchings.

The diverse application forms of Petri nets are indicated by their own references. A common breakdown consists of four classes of Petri nets (see *Peterson, Petri Net Theory and the Modelling of Systems 1981; Baumgarten, Petri-Netze 1990*):

- channel-instance net,
- condition-event net,
- position-transition net,
- predicate-transition net.

The simplest form of the Petri net is the channel-instance net (see Fig. B.II.66). It shows the components from which a system is constructed and which connections exist between the components. The boxes (squares) indicate active elements, which carry out functions such as creation, transporting or updating. Passive components are represented by circles. They describe system conditions, e. g. by specifying stocks on hand. The arrows indicate logical connections between instances and channels. The arrows lead either from instances to channels or from channels to instances. Channels and arrows describe paths within the net.

The transition from a static to a dynamic description is achieved by representing condition changes. Fig. B.II.67 illustrates this by way of a position-transition net. The boxes are now referred to as transitions and the circles as positions. Each position possesses a capacity specification (K=), each arrow a weight, and each position a start marker which is shown as a point within a circle. The starting level of the markers is only allowed to be as large as the relevant capacities. By activating a transition a change in condition is achieved. A switch reduces the number of the markers at each preceding position by the number of the arrow weighting between this position and the transition. At the same time the marker number is increased at each subsequent position by the number of the arrow weighting between the transition and this position (see the example of the switching process in Fig. B.II.67).

The representation can be refined in a predicate-transition net, in that various marker types (individual markers) are introduced. Markers with various characteristics (predicates) can then be used to indicate different products or orders, for example.

Fig. B.II.68 gives a rough meta-structure for Petri nets. The various classes of nets are represented by the entity type NET CLASS, the various types of node (active or passive, or represented by boxes or circles) by the entity type NODE TYPE. A node is specified by the link between NET CLASS and NODE TYPE. An edge (arrow) is a link between two nodes.

Using diverse switching operations a node can assume various conditions. This is indicated by the relationship type SWITCH CONDITION.

With the help of Petri nets, functions and data can be represented simultaneously. Of course, the emphasis on functions is stronger. Instances relate to functions or events. In the ARIS architecture events are rather described as data elements. For this reason, instances can relate to elements of both a function model and a data model. Channels represent conditions and thus tend to relate to data elements.

Organizational units are described by the representation of capacities, so that all ARIS components are in principle capable of being modelled in Petri nets. An application-specific example of modelling CIM systems is given by Busch (see *Busch, Entwurf eines Systems zur integrierten Fertigung 1989*).

The meta-structure of the Petri nets is not used further below.

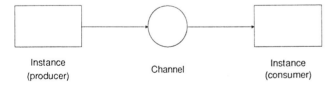

Instance (producer)    Channel    Instance (consumer)

Fig. B.II.66: Channel-instance net

134

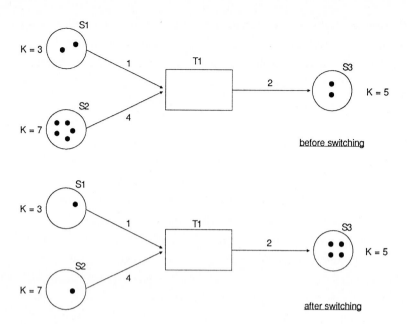

Fig. B.II.67: Position-transition net

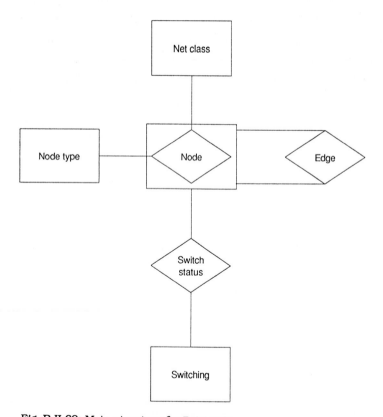

Fig. B.II.68: Meta-structure for Petri nets

**B.II.4.1.5 The Requirements Definition - Control Model**

The information model developed for the control modelling is summarized in Fig. B.II.69.

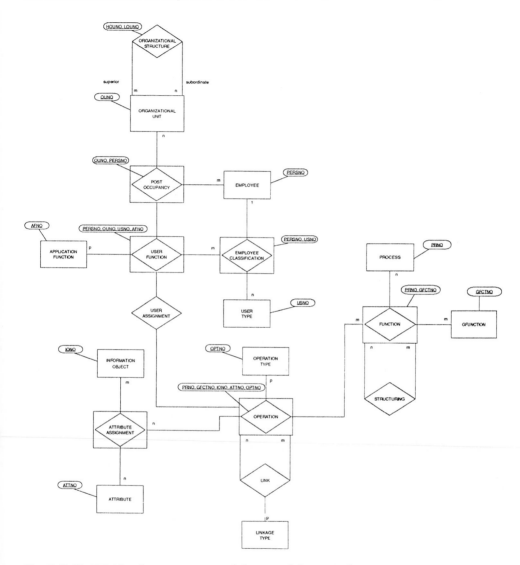

Fig. B.II.69: ERM for the requirements definition of the control view

### B.II.4.2 Procedural Model for Control Modelling

In order to avoid repetition of the description of the procedural models for the other views, the discussion will be kept brief. A procedural model for the SADT technique has already been discussed in the function modelling. Fig. B.II.70, therefore, aims to give an impression of the possibilities of powerful "front end" tools, which allow different views to be either separated or amalgamated using window techniques.

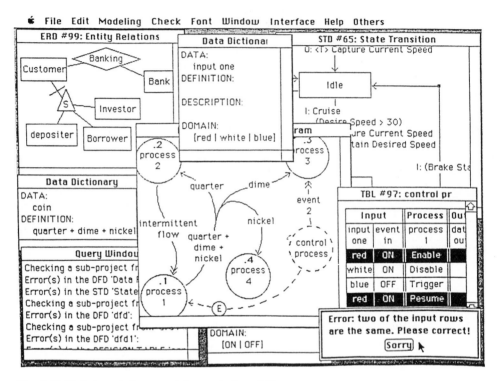

Fig. B.II.70: Integrated support for control modelling
(Screen form from the CASE tool "TurboCASE" from StructSoft Inc.)

See, for example, *Schönthaler, INCOME und CASE* 1990* for tool support of Petri nets using the tool INCOME.

### B.III  Design Specification

The requirements definitions are not transferred directly to the implementation level, but are transformed, as an intermediate step, into design specifications.

Whereas the requirements definition is a creative process, the transformation is more of a technical procedure which adapts the existing contents to the requirements of the information and communication techniques. This transformation should retain the content of the requirements definition. The main criterion for this design step is therefore the efficiency of the system being created. Typical principles formulationg this goal in concrete terms during the design specification phase are: abstraction, structuring, modularising, the information hiding principle, the principle of functional and informal links, the principle of narrow data links, and the principle of interface specification (see *Balzert, Die Entwicklung von Software-Systemen 1982, p. 190; Gabriel, Software Engineering 1990, p. 266 ff.*).

Whereas a transformation process thus occurs between the development phases in which the result of the previous phase is adapted to new side constraints, within a design phase an expansion resulting from detailing occurs. Nevertheless, it is always the same problem that is being considered, even if from different perspectives and thus in different languages. This "phase-uniformity" does not necessarily follow the procedural concept of the waterfall model, but rather the phases correspond to specific ways of representing the problem. These can also arise in cyclical form as a spiral model or in the framework of a prototyping approach. The important point is that the different phases should be defined in terms of their goals, representational methods and results. Even the use of generative tools does not make the phase definition superfluous. Precisely because of the phase-specific goals, simulations can be helpful in the use of generators, in that various implementation alternatives can be analyzed, e. g. transformation of a function of the requirements definition first into a module, and then into transactions of the design specification. These possibilities are also facilitated by the use of prototypes.

The information technology requirements are taken into account in the design specification phase only in general form, i. e., they are not yet derived from concrete hardware or software products.

The design specification phase, therefore, fulfills a buffer function between the application level and the computer-technical implementation. It is more formal than the requirements definition, but is not yet linked to concrete computer-technical hardware and software components. The connection between the design specification phase and implementation is closer than that between the requirements definition and the design specification, however (see Fig. A.II.03).

The justification for the intermediate level results from the fact that new objectives arise over and above those of the requirements definition. Whereas in the requirements definition only the semantic factors are represented, restrictions and objectives of the information technology now have to be incorporated. These relate to performance considerations, avoidance of redundancies and anomalies in typical data processing operations such as the creation, addition or updating of data, for example.

Given these various objectives, Balzert, for example (see *Balzert, Die Entwicklung von Software-Systemen 1982, pp. 188*), doubts whether automatic transfer of information from the requirements definition to the design specification phase is possible. Instead, only a selective transfer of definition characteristics in the product design is considered feasible. This view seems too pessimistic, though. The more semantically unambiguous languages and graphical constructs are available for the requirements definition level, the more results can be transformed by formal procedures. With the help of generators this can even be carried out automatically. This is already in practical use, for example, with respect to the semantic data model. But for the other views, too, the use of generators is increasingly being discussed, and tools are increasingly being offered (see, e. g., the tool Excelerator with the X-Tract component for generating different program codes).

The data, function and organization objects established in the requirements definition are transformed into other constructs within the design specification. The relationships of these objects are expressed in Fig. B.III.01 in that independent terms at both levels are permitted, insofar as they are typical of, and also introduced at, this level; at the same time, however, the terms are linked together by (transformation) relationships.

In the breakdown of the discussion of the design specification the views of the ARIS architecture are again followed.

In order to avoid repetition, the representation of the procedural model is omitted.

Fig. B.III.01: Link between requirements definition and desing specification

### B.III.1 Design Specification of the Function View

The incorporation of the design step "design specification of the function view" is shown in Fig. B.III.02. The design specification for functions can be carried out in various stages of a "top-down process". It is also referred to as **software design**, since the functions are subsequently implemented in program structures. The term "large scale programming" is also common, whereas the later implementation in a programming language is referred to as "small scale programming" (see *Balzert, Die Entwicklung von Software-Systemen 1982, p. 186; Gabriel, Software Engineering 1990, p. 266*). Essential design steps are the linking of software components with the elements of the requirements definition, the design of the module structure, the formulation of a detailed design for the module contents and the output of results. This process is reflected in the breakdown into:

- module design,
- control structures,
- presentation of output.

Since functions transform input data into output data, the link with the data view is particularly close. At the same time the information technology restrictions are also taken into account in the context of the design specification.

These links are weakened by the pursuance of the abstraction principle, so that the function concept can be created with no knowledge of the data model or a concrete hardware architecture. The abstraction principle restricts the analysis to the relevant components of the segment of reality. This means that only general properties of the neighbouring architectural blocks are considered, but not their specific instances. This is made clear by data abstraction, for example, in which only the data type is established, but not its physical implementation. For example, the data element "customer number" can be defined as an integer type for interface description purposes, without requiring details of the carrier of this data element, e. g. the entity type CUSTOMER as defined in the data model context, or its database-technical implementation by the specification of relation name, record type, or even record address and field indicator. The same applies to the hardware components, for example, a virtual terminal with basic properties is defined for the functional description of screen forms, without the need for reference to a specific class of devices.

The abstraction principle is also applied within the function description, in that, at first, in the course of the model design, the algorithmic representation of the procedural contents is abstracted from (at the same time the hiding principle is applied), whereas

140

later, in the detailed design, the specification of the algorithmic process is presented in greater detail.

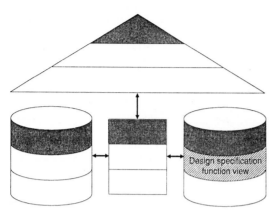

Fig. B.III.02: Incorporation of the design specification of the function view in ARIS

### B.III.1.1 Module Design

The module is a central element of the software design. It refers to an independent functional block with defined entry and exit. A module consists of data declaration, control logic and instructions. The creation of modules supports the principle of locality and reusability, since modules can be employed for different application functions. By defining entry and exit points, which are primarily made available to the user, the principle of "information hiding" is adopted. "What" a module does is described, but not "how".

Modules should be designed such that their intra-action is high, but the inter-action between modules is low (the principle of narrow data coupling). The design of modules can be effected in both top-down and bottom-up approaches. In the top-down approach the design is initiated at the highest level, and then refined until basic modules are formed, which can be implemented using the fundamental constructs of the basic software.

In the bottom-up approach, in contrast, modules are designed at the lowest level and amalgamated into modules at the next level up. The bottom-up design is particularly suitable when a complete product archive already exists, from which the basic modules can be taken and combined into larger units (see *Balzert, Die Entwicklung von Software Systemen 1982, p. 262 ff.*).

The term procedure is also used for modules; modules at a higher level are referred to as programs.

The level of the requirements definition can be adopted for these design approaches, since here too both bottom-up and top-down procedures are possible. The function hierarchy developed there thus provides the starting point for the module creation. In Fig. B.III.03 the term general function "GFUNCTION" is selected as the starting point. General function was used to refer to a function description which is still independent of any specific business process. This gives additional prominence to the principle of repeated application which should be applied in module creation.

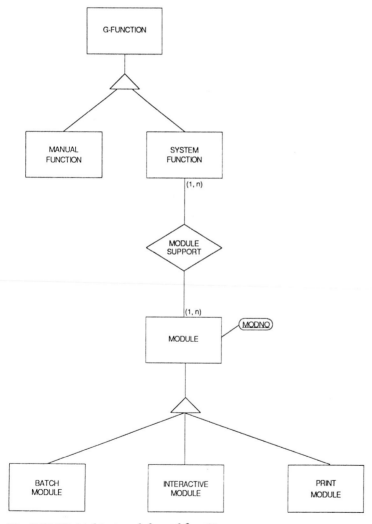

Fig. B.III.03: Linking module and function

Since modules are only created for computerized functions, a relationship with the specialized entity type SYSTEM FUNCTION is generated. The n:m relationship with a lower limit of 1 implies that a module (on the basis of repeated application) can be employed in various system functions, and a system function can be supported by various modules. In addition, the n:m relationship between system function and module also indicates that a certain independence exists between the requirements definition and the design specification.

A module can be specialized into sub-types.

Modules can be linked together in a network using call-up relationships. A self-explanatory example of a structure diagram is shown in Fig. B.III.04. The modules are represented by boxes. Pre-defined modules which can be already accessed from the outset are indicated by double side lines.

The graphical representation using structure diagrams is based especially on the work of Constantine and Jourdan on "Composite/Structured Design" (see *Page-Jones, The Practical Guide to Structured System Design 1980; Balzert, Die Entwicklung von Software-Systemen 1982*; see also *Sommerville, Software Engineering 1987, p. 83 ff., p. 91 ff.*).

Connectors (see Fig. B.III.04) abridge the representation. The communication between modules is indicated by arrows with data specifications. The arrow shown in the diagram indicates a pure data link. In addition, control links and transient parameters (parameters which have both input and output characteristics) are also possible. With extensive data relationships these can be numbered and relocated in a table.

The connectors A, B and C refer to data management access operations and constitute a data abstraction, i. e. identify data with the operations carried out on them.

The black rhombus beneath the module "handle sale" indicates the control structure "selection".

The hierarchy between modules is generated by the direction of call-ups. The hierarchically higher module calls up the lower level module. The direction of the call-up is expressed by the direction of the arrows between the modules.

The module hierarchy must be created in accordance with a uniform criterion: a relation. Examples of such a relation are "calls up" or "has as a component". In a call-up hierarchy a module executes a part of the task using its own program code, the remainder by calling up functions of another module (see *Lockemann/Dittrich, Architektur von Datenbanksystemen 1987, p. 102*). A component hierarchy simply fills the pages of the hierarchy module with instructions. This means that the call-up relations in a

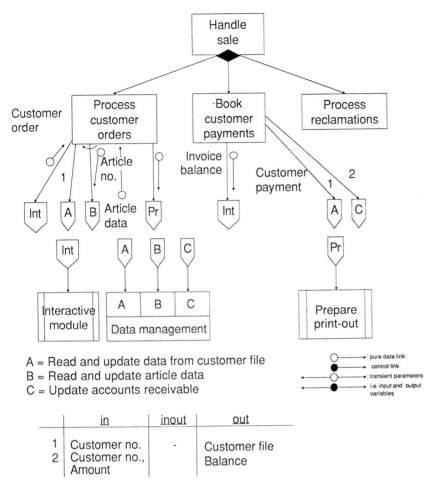

A = Read and update data from customer file
B = Read and update article data
C = Update accounts receivable

○——→ : pure data link
●——→ : control link
◐——→ : transient parameters
●——→ : i.e. input and output variables

|   | in | inout | out |
|---|---|---|---|
| 1 | Customer no. | – | Customer file |
| 2 | Customer no., Amount | | Balance |

Fig. B.III.04: Module representation using structure diagram

from: *Balzert, Die Entwicklung von Software-Systemen 1982, p. 356*

component hierarchy are not immediately obvious. See *Lockemann/Dittrich, Architektur von Datenbanksystemen 1987, p. 103* on the individual module breakdown steps.

The module classification, e. g. by sub-division into data manipulation, processing or interactive modules, is generated in Fig. B.III.05 by a 1:n relationship between the entity types MODULE and MODULE TYPE.

The relationships existing between modules are indicated in Fig. B.III.05 by the relationship type COMMUNICATION. The entity type COMMUNICATION TYPE indicates the kind of link, i. e. a pure data link, for example, or a control link. The data exchanged

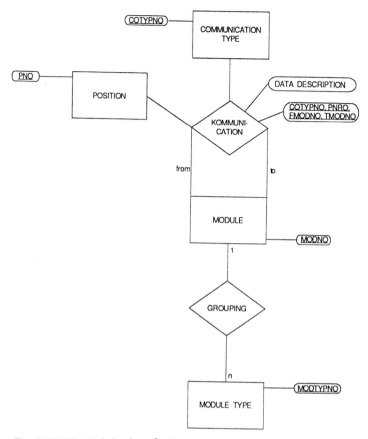

Fig. B.III.05: Module classification

are themselves shown as the attribute "data description". If each communication relationship can carry only one datum then position numbers can be assigned for communication sets. This formally links the relationship type with the entity type POSITION.

A further sub-division of modules can be generated using the menu technique.
A menu presents the user a choice of application transactions within a given area. (see Fig. B.III.06).
A menu call-up can itself be an application transaction.
Since the term module also incorporates the term interactive module, that is the user transaction, menu control is already represented in Fig. B.III.05 by the relationship type COMMUNICATION.

```
┌─────────────────────────────────────────────────────────────────────┐
│  Command                    MENU: AMBM10                      IN      │
│                                                                       │
│                   ORDER RECORDING AND INVOICING                       │
│                          Process order                                │
│                                                                       │
│             1   Record order                                          │
│             2   Record order and release immediately                  │
│             3   Administer order                                      │
│             4   Release order                                         │
│             5   Record order on diskette                              │
│             6   Update segment                                        │
│             7   Packing label                                         │
│             8   Order confirmation                                    │
│             9   Invoices                                              │
│            10   Delivery notes                                        │
│            11   Return to main menu                                   │
│                                                                       │
│                                                                       │
│  ENTER COMMAND OR SELECTION NUMBER ▮ __                               │
│                                                                       │
│                                                                       │
└─────────────────────────────────────────────────────────────────────┘
```

Fig. B.III.06: Example of a menu

Source: *IBM*

Although the representation using structure diagrams is only one method of system design, the ERM structure developed from it is so general that other methods can also be represented within this logic (see *Sommerville, Software Engineering 1987, p. 77 ff., p. 106,* for example, for further specification languages).

Parallel to the term "module", the term "program" is also used. In general, a program is "a complete set of instructions with all the necessary provisions for carrying out a task" (see *Stetter, Softwaretechnologie 1983, p. 15*).

If a program consists of program parts (sub-programs) which communicate with each other, this constitutes a program system. If the sub-programs fulfill the requirements on modules, it is referred to as modular. On the other hand, however, a module also fulfills the original definition of a program, so that a module can also be referred to as a program with special properties. For this reason, the parallel use of these terms is justified. Nevertheless, the explicit use of the term "program" tends to imply a combination of modules, that is, a framework for calling up modules.

The level of detail of the module design depends on the processing form. If interactive processing is being aimed at, then transactions or tasks are created. These constitute a coherent processing step on the part of a user. According to the degree of detail of the requirements definition, a task can correspond to the lowest hierarchy level of the conceptual breakdown (elementary function).

The level of detail of the breakdown of the design specification also depends on the EDP systems subsequently to be employed: Some transaction managers can best handle many small tasks, others a few large ones (see *Olle/Hagelstein/MacDonald: Information Systems 1988, p. 108*). These information technology influences should only be taken into account by the design specification in global form.

### B.III.1.2 Mini-Specification

The content of a module is described in a semi-formal manner in the context of the design specification, using mini-specifications. Typical methods are pseudo-code,

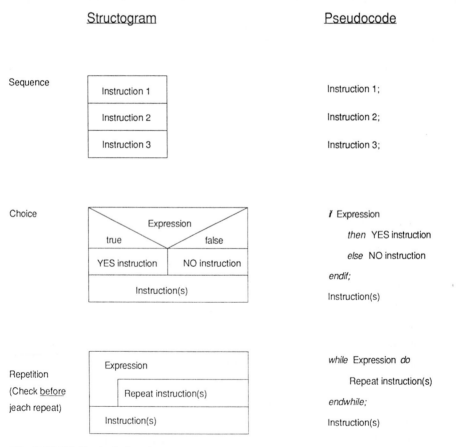

Fig. B.III.07: Control structures

decision tables or structograms. The subject matter of the description are both control structures, which control the process of an algorithm, and the executing instructions. Sequence, selection and repetition are employed as control structures. Fig. B.III.07 represents these in simple form using both structograms and pseudo-code.

The instructions consist of procedure or module call-ups and arithmetic operations. These operations are carried out at the data element level.

Depending on the level of complexity, the control structures can interlock within a module.

The most extensive description is given in the leaves of a module tree or module network, whereas at the higher levels the module contents consist essentially of control structures and call-up instructions.

Fig. B.III.08 represents the identification of a control structure by combination of the entity types CONTROL STRUCTURE TYPE, HIERARCHY LEVEL, and MODULE. Here, control structure incorporates the entire block of instructions. A module comprises several control structures which are assigned to various hierarchy levels. The instructions belonging to a control structure are represented in the form of a 1:n relationship.

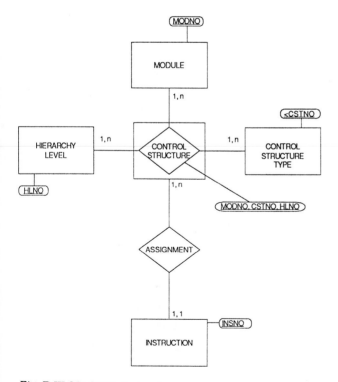

Fig. B.III.08: Control structure

148

## B.III.1.3  Output Presentation

The input and output rules are established in the construction of screen forms (primarily for online communication) and listings (primarily for batch processing). Fig. B.III.09 and Fig. B.III.10 present examples.

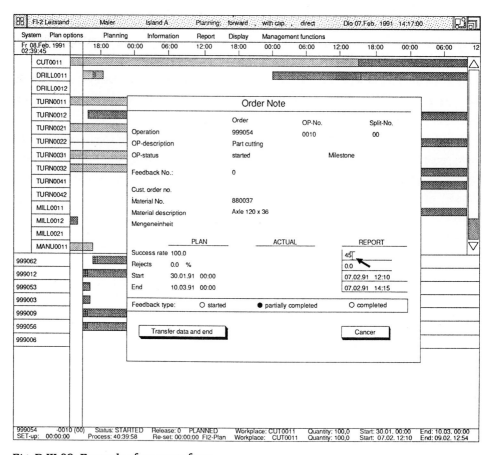

Fig. B.III.09: Example of a screen form

(user interface of the intelligent Leitstand A-2 of IDS Prof. Scheer GmbH)

Screen forms, or panels, can be used for both input and output. A panel type can be input or output by several modules. Therefore, in the ERM diagram in Fig. B.III.11 a cardinality of (0,n) is specified for both input and output functions. Since a panel type can be presented in several national languages, a specific panel is the result of combining language and panel type. A panel can be incorporated in an existing panel using the window technique, as shown in Fig. B.III.09. As a result, a relationship exists within the

| Job shop order | | | | Date: 01.02.91 | |
| CIM-TTZ | Nr.03 | | | Time: | 16:35 |

| Order | Part | Description | Quantity | Start | End |
|-------|-------|-------------|----------|-------|------|
| U03100 | 03434 | Quartz clock | 10 | 01.02. | 10.02 |

| Operations | Machine ID | Description | Processing time | Set-up time |
|------------|------------|-------------|-----------------|-------------|
| 10 | Drill01 | Drill | 15 min | 3 min |
| 20 | Mill03 | Mill | 25 min | 5 min |
| 30 | Ass02 | Assemble | 5 min | 1 min |
| 40 | Qual04 | | | |

Fig. B.III.10: Example of a listing

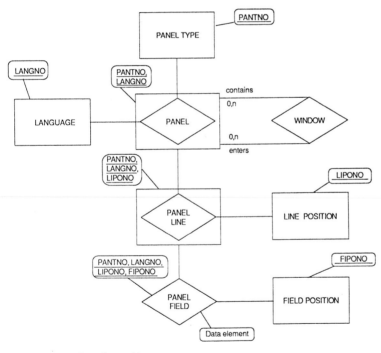

Fig. B.III.11: Panel creation

reinterpreted entity type PANEL. Different lines can be defined within a panel, which are interpreted as the link between the line position and the panel. Essential attributes of the panel line are text characters. The individual fields in which data are input or output are created as panel fields in combination with the entity type FIELD POSITION. Panels can be interpreted as views of the data model. This will be considered further in the discussion of the control concept.

The list header of output listings can be interpreted in a nearly analogous manner (Fig. B.III.12). One difference from the panel definition is that listings are only used for output. The individual listing positions are not considered further in the ERM, since they merely constitute instances, just as the individual panel instances are not indicated in Fig. B.III.11, only the formatted structure. The terms PANEL FIELD and LIST FIELD introduced as relationship types, are placed in their relation to the data view in the

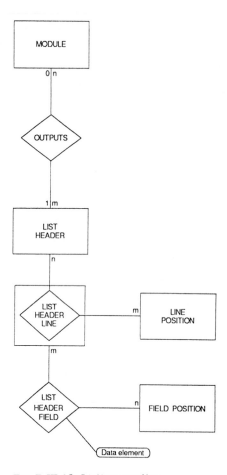

Fig. B.III.12: Listing creation

context of the control view of the design specification. At the same time panels and listings will be linked with the organization view in terms of those receiving or authorized to make inputs.

## B.III.2  Design Specification of the Organization View

The incorporation of this section is shown in Fig. B.III. 13

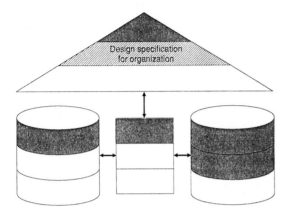

Fig. B.III.13: Incorporating the design specification of the organization view in ARIS

In the context of the requirements definition of the organization view, the organizational units of an enterprise, including their relationships with each other, were established. In considering the links between the organization and the other architectural blocks (control view) planning levels were defined, along with their functional assignments and their responsibility for data stocks.

The design specification transforms the requirements definition of the organization view into the topology of the data processing system. This means that the essential requirements for the structure of the computer network are derived from the application requirements.

Specifically, the network topology must, in addition to meeting general capacity requirements, establish the kind of user access to individual nodes and the kind of components needed to provide this.

## B.III.2.1 Network Topology

Fig. B.III.14 shows a typical network configuration for an industrial firm. It contains various network topologies (star network, ring network, and bus; see Fig. B.III.15).

In addition to the topology of the network, in which certain properties concerning the failure of the network, speed, and access to the network are expressed (see *Hutchinson/Marian/Shephard, Local Area Networks 1985; Löffler, Lokale Netze 1988; Sikora/Steinparz, Computer & Kommunikation 1988; Sloman/Kramer, Verteilte Systeme und Rechnernetze 1988; Tannenbaum, Computer Networks 1988; Zieher, Kopplung von Rechnernetzen 1989*), networks can also be characterized in terms of other properties. For example, it is possible to distinguish between Wide Area Networks (WANs), which link spatially distant locations, and Local Area Networks (LANs), which link nodes within a single location.

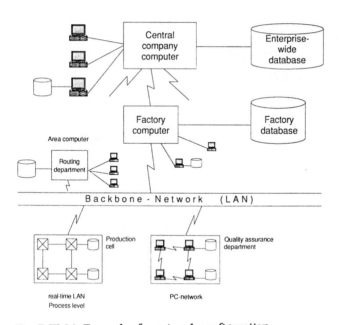

Fig. B.III.14: Example of a network configuration

Depending on the kind of devices to be included in the network, it is also possible to distinguish between a pure terminal network, which links terminals with a (host) computer, and networks which link intelligent workstations with each other.

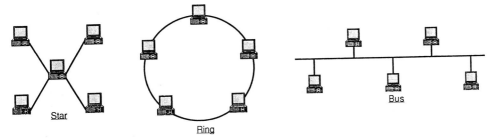

Fig. B.III.15: Network topologies

A backbone network forms the backbone link between networks with different properties. An important property is the real-time capability, for example, which is indicated particularly by transfer speed and network access control. A further, more technically-oriented view is the protocol selected for a network. Here, a distinction can be drawn between the token principle and the CSMA-CD principle, for example.

Establishing these properties of a network architecture is still independent of the concrete hardware products or concrete control software. It is based principally on the demands of the requirements definition.

Although various criteria can be used to describe the properties of networks, the single term "NETWORK TYPE" is introduced in Fig. B.III.16 to differentiate between the various network types. If necessary, this term can later be specialized into the various criteria of topology forms and protocol types. The entity type NETWORK TYPE describes possible kinds of network, as is visually expressed in Fig. B.III.14.
The entity type NETWORK is formed for the specific networks.

In the context of the design specification only the logical network structure is considered. This does not involve consideration of how the network will physically be laid, so that the transfer medium, such as glass fibre or coaxial cable, is also not yet established, for example. These tasks belong to the subsequent implementation phase. The independence of the design specfication from the implementation phase is clear from the fact that different logical networks can be effected using the same physical transfer medium.

Since the term NETWORK TYPE covers several distinguishing criteria, it is permissible for a network to be assigned to various network types. A network can be defined by its nodes and edges.

154

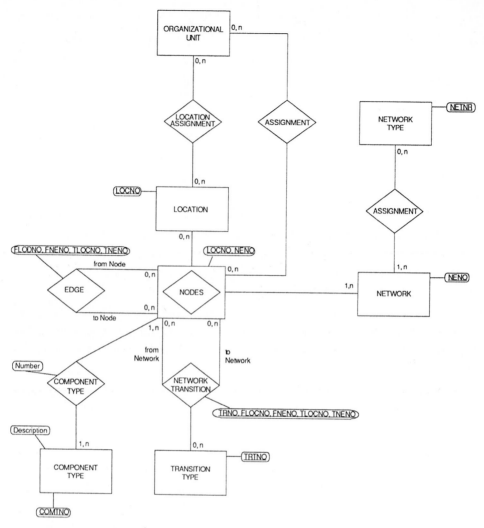

Fig. B.III.16: Network configuration

The physical location of a network node is indicated by the term LOCATION. (NETWORK) NODES is then a relationship type between LOCATION and NETWORK. A network consists of at least one and at most n nodes, and 0 or n different logical network nodes can be positioned at one location.

The topology of the network is expressed by the assignment relationships between the nodes. For this purpose, the relationship type EDGE is introduced between the reinterpreted entity type NODES.

0 or several edges can originate from one node, and 0 or several edges can lead to it. The case of 0 applies to a start or end node of a bus architecture. If transfer quantities are introduced as an attribute of the edge, then it makes sense to differentiate the edges in terms of their direction. This is indicated in the ERM representation by the role description "from" and "to".

Since an isolated consideration of the organization view, without reference to the design specification for functions and data, only allows global assessments of the transfer quantities, the important data sets to be transferred (e. g. article data or production orders) can be specified as attributes.

The networks defined for an organization do not generally exist in isolation, but are linked with each other. This also emerges for the configuration example of Fig. B.III.14.

Different forms of transition between networks exist, which are based on the level of the network protocol. If all levels of a network protocol (e. g. all seven layers of the ISO-OSI reference model) are translated from one network protocol into the protocol of another network this is referred to as a gateway between the networks. In contrast, if some levels (usually the upper levels) are already in conformity, so that only the protocols for the lower levels need to be translated, these forms are then implemented by routers and bridges. These kinds of links are characterized by the entity type TRANSITION TYPE in Fig. B.III.16.

The transition from one network to another network is effected by a link from one node of one network to another node of the other network. This is represented by the relationship type NETWORK TRANSITION, whose definition includes the transition type (gateway, router, etc.).

The relationship to the requirements definition for the organization structure and the network topology is generated by adopting the entity types LOCATION and ORGANIZATIONAL UNIT from the requirements definition. If responsibilities are defined at the node level, i. e. if several organizational units share one computer node or if a node in one location is available only to the organizational units that are in principle assigned to that location, then NODE ASSIGNMENT needs to be created between NODES and ORGANIZATIONAL UNIT. Fig B.III.16 also includes this relationship.

## B.III.2.2 Component Types

Thus far a node is merely defined by its location and the network to which it belongs. The kind of hardware installed is not yet specified. For example, it is not obvious whether a node consists of a complete computer system, simply an input or output station, or a decentralized workstation with access to background systems. This further specification can be achieved by introducing a node type into the node definition.

In order to describe the general types of devices, that is, whether complete computer systems or simply an output device are to be positioned at one node, the term COMPONENT TYPE is introduced. Various component types can be employed at a node. The typical attribute for a component type is its description.

The relationship type COMP.-ASSIGNMENT can be interpreted in different ways. If the node definition is so narrow that a device can be identified with each node, so that each terminal is also a node in the computer network, then from the node perspective there exists a (1,1) cardinality, i. e. a node is always assigned to precisely one component type. A component type, on the other hand, can be employed at several nodes.

However, if the node is merely interpreted as a point of access to a network which can be used by several devices such as terminals or output stations, for example, then several component types can also be employed at one node. The number of devices of one type to be used at one node is then held as an attribute of the assignment relationship.

## B.III.3 Design Specification of the Data View

The incorporation of this section is shown in Fig. B.III.17.

In the context of the design specification, the semantic data model of the requirements definition is translated into the language of the database system interface. Here, the database systems follow specific data models. However, these must be distinguished from the concept of the semantic data model. Currently commonplace are the hierarchical, network-oriented and relational data models. Since the hierarchical model is now only of historical interest, and the network-oriented model is also losing significance, the following treatment is exclusively in terms of the relational data model. The object-oriented data model is merely touched upon.

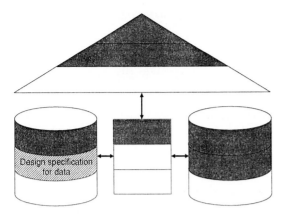

Fig. B.III.17: Incorporation of the design specification of the data view in ARIS

In the first step, the information objects of the requirements definition are transformed into relations. Fixed rules exist for this.

In the second step, the relations are submitted to an optimization process, in which a normalization process removes anomalies concerning the addition, updating or removal of tuples. As a result, "raw relations" taken over from the requirements definition can be broken down further. In the case of performance problems resulting from too fine breakdown of relations, the reverse process, that is a denormalization of the table, can also be undertaken.

In the third step, integrity conditions are defined. These can be adopted from the requirements definition and transformed into the notation of the relational model, or they can be newly introduced from the design specification perspective. The reformulation of integrity conditions already contained in the requirements definitions necessitated by the limited linguistic scope of the relational model, which merely recognizes tables, so that integrity conditions need to be formulated with the help of a data manipulation language.

In the fourth step, the relational schema is transformed into the data description language of a specific database management system. In this process logical access paths are added to support record-oriented processing. This last step constitutes the transition to the implementation phase and could also be regarded as the first step of that phase.

In the data description language (DDL) of a database system the relational schema is taken over and adapted to the formal requirements of the DDL. Thus, no implementation-related changes are made. At the same time, the DDL is the descriptive language which is closest to implementation, and in which the other views can communicate with the data view. Applications, therefore, should not communicate with the implementation level of the data view, but only via the database schema formulated in the DDL.

### B.III.3.1 Forming Relations

A relation Ri is defined by listing attribute names Aij (see (1) in Fig. B.III.18). A relation can be represented visually as a table. Mathematically, a relation is a subset of the Cartesian product of the domains assigned to the attributes (see (2) in Fig. B.III.18).

(1) $R_i$ $(A_{i1}, A_{i2}, \ldots, A_n)$

Part (Part number, Description, Stocks)

| Part | Part number | Description | Stocks |
|------|-------------|-------------|--------|
|      | 4717        | Screw       | 526    |
|      | 4728        | Bolt        | 768    |

(2) $R_i \subseteq D_{i1} \times D_{i2} \times \ldots \times D_n$
  whereby $D_i$ = domain of $A_i$

Fig. B.III.18: Representation of relations

The relations can be derived from the requirements definition formulated with the help of the ERM by applying relatively simple rules. Each entity type as well as each n:m relationship type becomes a relation (an n:m relationship type is recognizable by the fact that at least two cardinalities with respect to a bordering entity type display an upper limit of n). For 1:n relationship types no independent relation is generated, however, instead the relation is adopted into the entity type from which the cardinality with the upper limit of 1 originates by adoption of the key attribute (see the example in Fig. B.III.19). This adopted key attribute is referred to as a foreign key.

In the ERM representation of Fig. B.III.20 the entity type RELATION is first introduced with the key attribute RELNO. The relationship to the entity type INFORMATION OBJECT from the requirements definition is generated by the relationship GENERATION. Given the generation prescriptions, an information object can enter into 0 or at most 1 relations. A relation, however, can apply to one or more information objects.

ERM                                              Relations

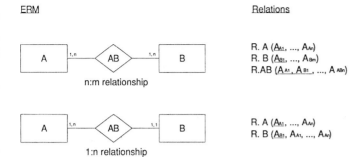

R. A ($\underline{A}_{A1}$, ..., $A_{An}$)
R. B ($\underline{A}_{B1}$, ..., $A_{Bm}$)
R.AB ($\underline{A_{A1}, A_{B1}}$, ..., $A_{ABn}$)

n:m relationship

R. A ($\underline{A}_{A1}$, ..., $A_{An}$)
R. B ($\underline{A}_{B1}$, $A_{A1}$, ..., $A_{An}$)

1:n relationship

Fig. B.III.19: Derivation of relations from the ERM

The entity type RELATION contains the relation name, which can also be the same as the name of the information object, as an attribute.

The attribute names which belong to a relation can also be taken over from the requirements definition. Of course, it is also possible to change the names from those used in the requirements definition. If no reformulations are made, however, the attributes are available directly from the link between RELATION and INFORMATION OBJECT. In order to emphasize the independence of the "design specification" level, however, the attributes assigned to the relation are introduced by means of the relationship type RELATION ATTRIBUTE ASSIGNMENT, which creates a link with the attribute assignment of the requirements definition.

If no names are changed in the takeover from the requirements definition, then the formation of the relations can be carried out quasi-automatically using the transformation rule. Many CASE tools offer this transfer step from an ERM representation in automated form.

With respect to the domains, the existing domain definitions of the requirements definition are accessed via the attribute assignments. For didactic reasons, the entity type DOMAIN, in close association with the relational model, will be given special consideration later in the treatment of the integrity conditions applying to domains.

Whereas the transfer of entity and relationship types into the relational model does not pose any difficulties, the transfer of complex objects into the relational model is more problematic. Here, extensions need to be undertaken in which procedures are adopted as attributes in the relational model, for example, or the data model is even taken in the direction of an object-oriented data model (see *Dittrich, Stand und Tendenzen der "nachrelationalen" Datenbanktechnologie 1990; Härder, Non-Standard-Datenbanksysteme 1990).*

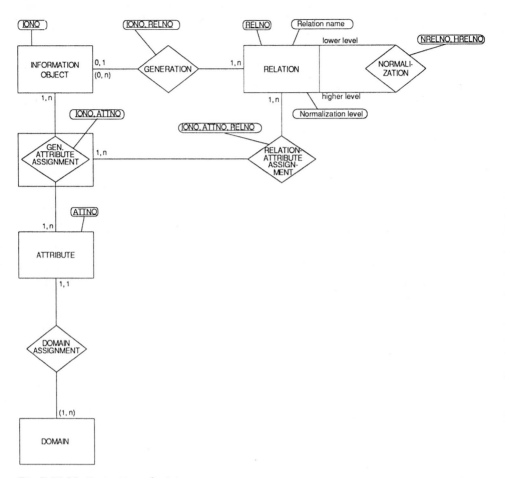

Fig. B.III.20: Derivation of relations

## B.III.3.2 Normalization - Denormalization

The "raw" relations taken over from the requirements definition can give rise to unwanted effects in the general database functions: insertion, deletion, updating, which can impair the consistency of the database schema. These effects are referred to as anomalies, which are to be reduced via the normalization process. The normalization process was certainly developed in connection with the relational model, but it can be regarded as a general procedure for improving data structures, and is thus also applicable to other data models. The individual normalization stages are simply referred to as definitions; for a more complete treatment see the literature on database systems (see e. g. *Schlageter/Stucky, Datenbanksysteme 1983, p. 183 ff.; Wedekind, Datenbanksysteme I 1981, p. 200 ff.*). Furthermore, only the 1st to 3rd normal forms will be considered, the so-called Boyce/Codd normal form and the 4th and higher normal forms will not be included on the grounds of their rarity. The normalization process is illustrated using an example (see *Schlageter/Stucky, Datenbanksysteme 1983, p. 162*):

1. NF;

(\*,1)   EMP (<u>EMPNO</u>, NAME, ADDRESS, OCCUPATION, DEPT.NO)

(\*,2)   PROJECT (<u>PRNO</u>, PRNAME, PRDESCR; PR-LEADER)

(\*,3)   EMP-PROJ (<u>PRNO</u>, <u>EMPNO</u>, TELNO, PROC-WORKTIME)

(\*,4)   DEPARTMENT (<u>DEPTNO</u>, DEPT-HEAD, AREANO, STEWARD)

2. NF

(\*,5)   EMP-PROJ (<u>PRNO</u>, <u>EMPNO</u>, PROC-WORKTIME)

(\*,6)   AT (<u>EMPNO</u>, TELNO) -> in (1,1)

3. NF

in (1,4) STEWARD is transitively dependent on DEPTNO

DEPTNO ⇄ AREANO ⟶ STEWARD

(\*,7)   BUILDING (<u>BUILDINGNO</u>, STEWARD)

(\*,8)   DEPARTMENT\* (<u>DEPTNO</u>, DEPT-HEAD, BUILDINGNO)

**Definitions**

A relation R is in first normal form (1 NF) if each attribute value is elementary.

A relation R is in second normal form (2 NF) if it is in 1 NF and each non-key attribute is fully functionally dependent on each key candidate.

A relation R is in third normal form (3 NF) if it is in 2 NF and no non-key attributes are transitively dependent on a key candidate.

The example illustrating the execution of the normalization process relates to the data structure of a project organization.

The anomalies to be removed by the normalization process are demonstrated using 1 NF of the example.

An **insertion** anomaly arises, for example, when a new employee is placed in the database who has not yet been assigned to any project. It is then impossible to assign him a telephone number, since the attribute TELNO is only contained in the employee (EMP-)PROJECT relation.

A **deletion** anomaly arises when a project is completed and therefore the relation (1,3) is deleted. This means that the employee's telephone number is deleted, although it continues to apply to him.

An **update** anomaly is one in which changing the telephone number of one employee involves examining all the tuples of the relation EMP-PROJECT and having to change all employees' telephone numbers, who might be employed on several projects, even though only **one** fact has been altered.

If a relation is not altered in the course of the next normalization step, then only the attribute of the normalization level is increased. In the example the relations (*,1) and (*,2) are already in third normal form.

In formal terms, the normalization process leads to a further breakdown of the starting relations. How far this breakdown process is carried out depends on the condition of the starting relations. If a so-called universal relation, which is held in an unorganized form in the requirements definiton, is chosen as the start, then the normalization process leads to a comprehensive restructuring. However, if the design has already been carried out carefully, e. g. with the help of the entity-relationship model, then in general the information objects will already exist at a higher normalization stage.

However, since the normalization process relates above all to the non-key attributes, or to the relationship of non-key attributes to key attributes, then even in the case of careful design of information objects, whereby only the key attributes are defined in the first step, the non-key attributes being added at a later stage, useful checks can be made by applying the normalization process.

With respect to the introduced RELATION entity type, the breakdown process of normalization means that further relations are derived from the "raw relations" that have been adopted. These are also unambiguously identifiable by their key attribute, the relation number RELNO. Since an information object can lead to several relations, the cardinality of the relationship type GENERATION is altered to (0,n), as is already shown in brackets under the relevant edge in Fig. B.III.20.

The normalization stage can be held as an attribute of a relation.

The origin of a relation in a relation of a previous normalization stage is indicated by the relationship type NORMALIZATION. For a relation at a certain (higher) level this indicates from which relation at the lower normalization stage it is derived. In the example this is indicated by the numbering, since the first number in brackets indicates the number of origin and the second number the number of the relations. The brackets thus indicate the key attributes of the relationship type NORMALIZATION.

By forming new relations in the course of the normalization process the attribute assignments are changed from those of the requirements definition and hence also from those of the initially created raw relations. This does not lead to an extension of the ERM model in Fig. B.III.20, however, but only to the creation of new tuples of the relationship type RELATION-ATTRIBUTE ASSIGNMENT.

The data management of the standard software family of the software house SAP AG is based on a performance-oriented data organization.

The information objects with their attributes are defined in an SAP table. For each attribute (field) the attribute name (field name), key properties, type, length, assignment to a domain and a short description are given (see Fig. B.III.21 "Total costs are dependent on output CSIL" from the cost accounting system RK). The properties of an attribute are indicated up to the double line in the table.

The lines of the table are therefore equivalent to the columns of a table in the relational data model sense. These then contain the instances (tuples) of the information objects as lines.

Depending on the relevance of the key attributes, tuples of several information objects can be contained in a table of instances, and an information object can occur in several SAP tables.

In Fig. B.III.21 four information objects can be recorded which are indicated by different key combinations. These are shown at the right beyond the double line. The information objects are numbered in the columns. The crosses indicate whether an attribute applies as a key for the information object. The information objects have the following meanings:

```
                    R/3-Data Dictionary Infosystem (DD03P)

-------------------------------------------------------------------------
        Table name....... : CSIL
-------------------------------------------------------------------------
```

|  |  |  |  |  |  |  | Information object | | | |
|---|---|---|---|---|---|---|---|---|---|---|
| Field name | Key | Dat-Elem. | Type | Len | Domain | Short desription | 1 | 2 | 3 | 4 |
| _MANDT | X | MANDT | CHAR | 0003 | MANDT | Client | x | x | x | x |
| _WRTTP | X | WRTTP | NUMC | 0002 | WRTTP | Value type | x | x | - | x |
| _VERSN | X | VERSN | NUMC | 0003 | VERSN | Version number/plan variant | x | x | x | x |
| _KOKRS | X | KOKRS | CHAR | 0004 | CACCD | Cost centre group | x | x | x | x |
| _GJAHR | X | GJAHR | NUMJ | 0004 | GJAHR | Business year | x | x | x | x |
| _KOSTL | X | KOSTL | CHAR | 0010 | KOSTL | Cost centre | x | x | x | x |
| _LSTAR | X | LSTAR | CHAR | 0006 | LSTAR | Performance type | x | - | - | x |
| _KSTAR | X | KSTAR | CHAR | 0010 | SAKNR | Cost type | x | x | x | x |
| _PRTNR | X | PRTNR | CHAR | 0010 | PTRNR | Partner number | x | x | x | - |
| _TWAER | X | RTCUR | CUKY | 0005 | WAERS | Currency key | x | x | x | x |
| _MEINS | X | MEINS | UNIT | 0003 | MEINS | Basic quantity units | x | x | x | x |
| _BEKNZ | X | BEKNZ | CHAR | 0001 | BEKNZ | Debit/Credit indicator | x | x | x | x |
| _PERBL | X | RPMAX | CHAR | 0003 | RPMAX | Maximum period | x | x | x | x |
| _IGF01 |  | IGFXX | CURR | 0015 | CVAL8 | Actual costs split |  |  |  |  |
| _IGF02 |  | IGFXX | CURR | 0015 | CVAL8 | Actual costs split |  |  |  |  |
| _IGF03 |  | IGFXX | CURR | 0015 | CVAL8 | Actual costs split |  |  |  |  |
| _IGF04 |  | IGFXX | CURR | 0015 | CVAL8 | Actual costs split |  |  |  |  |
| _IGF05 |  | IGFXX |  |  |  |  |  |  |  |  |
| _IGF06 |  |  |  |  |  |  |  |  |  |  |
| _IGF |  |  |  |  |  |  |  |  |  |  |

Fig. B.III.21: Example of performance-oriented data organization

source: *SAP AG*

NR. Name of the information object

1. Secondary Production Output Allocation

The secondary production output allocations are the value of the exchange of services from one cost centre to another cost centre at the end of the period.

2. Cost Centre Accounting

Cost centre accounting is the specification of the costs of one cost centre for one cost unit at the end of the period.

3. Performance-Related Planned Cost Variations

The performance-related planned cost variations indicate which costs a cost centre plans to use for a certain cost type in order to achieve a specific planned performance in the period.

4. Cumulative Charges and Discharges for a Cost Centre

The cumulative charges and discharges for a cost centre contain the total values of all discharges and charges of a cost centre, differentiated by cost type and performance type for the period.

### B.III.3.3 Integrity Conditions

Consideration of the integrity conditions ensures that the database always presents an accurate representation of reality (see *Blaser/Jarke/Lehmann, Datenbanksprachen und Datenbankbenutzung 1987, p. 586*). In the context of the requirements definition, integrity conditions have already been established. These include the cardinalities, the definition of so-called weak entity types, and the domain definition.

Since the tabular representation of the relational model offers only limited possibilities for defining semantic subject matter, the integrity conditions are defined in a data manipulation language (DML). Naturally, integrity conditions can also be formulated within an application program. However, it is in accordance with the principle of locality, and also with the advantages of the central control of data integrity, to formulate these conditions in the context of the data view. It should be noted, however, that, given the close links between the data and the function views and the resulting arbitrary divisions, both possibilities exist. This also explains the "tug of war" between the views. "Active" databases demand, for example, that as much as possible of the functionality that was once part of the programm systems be relocated in the database environment (see *Dittrich, Stand und Tendenzen der "nachrelationalen" Datenbanktechnologie 1990*, for example).

Integrity conditions relate on the one hand to the security of the semantic contents of the data model, but also to the underlying implementation levels. However, the conditions are a fixed part of the database systems, so that they are not the subject of the user's design decisions. For this reason, the semantic integrity conditions occupy the foreground here.

Consistency conditions relate to attributes, relation instances (tuples) and relations arising out of relationship types (see *Blaser/Jarke/Lehmann, Datenbanksprachen und Datenbankbenutzung 1987, p. 588 ff.*). Conditions concerning relationship types are also referred to as referential integrity conditions.

The standard data manipulation language of the relational model is SQL. In SQL integrity conditions are defined by asserting instructions and by the execution of actions on the basis of some event trigger.

For example, if it is necessary to ensure that in an EMPLOYEE relation the deletion of a personnel number (PERSNO) also initiates the deletion of the reference in the POSSESSES relation which generates the link with the SKILL relation, this can be achieved by the following trigger definition (see *Blaser/Jarke/Lehmann, Datenbanksprachen und Datenbankbenutzung 1987, p. 592*):

DEFINE TRIGGER T1

ON DELETE OF EMPLOYEE (PERSNO):

DELETE POSSESSES

WHERE POSSESSES.PERSNO = EMPLOYEE.PERSNO

Examples of assert formulations are summarized in Fig. B.III.22

| Explanation | SQL - Formulation |
|---|---|
| 1) The condition relates to an attribute. Examples are: Instances of PERS-NO must be 4-digit numbers. | ASSERT IB1 ON EMPLOYEE: PERS-NO BETWEEN 0001 AND 9999 |
| 2) The condition relates to the several attributes of a record instance. An example is: TOTAL WAGES in a department must be less than its ANNUAL BUDGET. | ASSERT IB2 ON DEPARTMENT: TOTAL WAGES < ANNUAL BUDGET |
| 3) The condition relates to several instances of the same record type (relation). Examples are: No employee's wage may be more than 20 % above the average wage of all employees in the same department. | ASSERT IB3 ON EMPLOYEE X: WAGE $\leq$ 1.2 * (SELECT AVG (WAGE)) FROM EMPLOYEE WHERE DEPT.MEMB.=X.DEPT.MEMB.) |
| 4) The condition relates to several instances from various relations. An example is: The value of TOTAL WAGES of a department must always be the same as the sum of the WAGE fields of its employee's. | ASSERT IB4 ON DEPARTMENT X: TOTAL WAGES = (SELECT SUM (WAGE) FROM EMPLOYEE WHERE DEPT.MEMB.=X.DEPT.NO.) |

Fig. B.III.22: Integrity conditions

from: *Reuter, Sicherheits- und Integritätsbedingungen 1987, p. 381, 385*

Fig. B.III.23 presents the essential interdependences in the linking up of integrity conditions. The left side of Fig. B.III.23 with the entity types RELATION, ATTRIBUTE and DOMAIN is the starting point for the integrity analysis. The entity type INTEGRITY TYPE describes various kinds of integrity conditions (see *Reuter, Sicherheits- und*

*Integritätsbedingungen 1987, p. 380 ff.*). They vary in terms of their scope (determination of the type and number of objects which are covered by an integrity condition; examples are given in Fig. B.III.22), in terms of the time at which they are checked (whether they are carried out continuously or only after a certain number of operations have been handled), in terms of the type of check that is made (whether status conditions or transition conditions) and in terms of whether actions (triggers) are initiated in connection with the integrity condition.

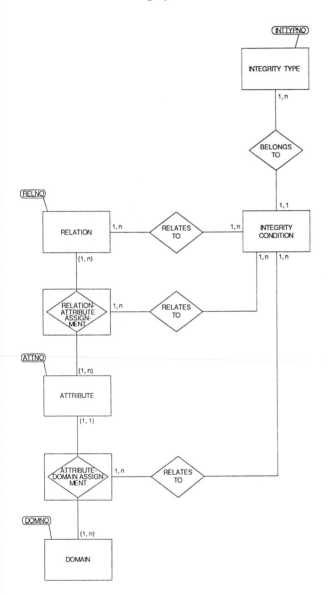

Fig. B.III.23 Integrity conditions

Each specific integrity condition is assigned in Fig. B.III.23 to an integrity type. An integrity condition can refer to one or more relations.

An integrity condition can refer to attribute assignments of one or more relations.

Checking of the attribute value limits is generated by the link with the attribute domain assignment.

### B.III.3.4 Logical Access Paths

The execution of interdependent SQL queries can give rise to considerable performance problems. In order to improve the efficiency of the database, help structures are therefore created which support access to the individual tuples or sets of tuples. In particular, it is necessary to ensure that tables do not have to be searched sequentially.

Typical aids relate to the accessing of a tuple using its key, and the accessing of sets of tuples in a certain processing sequence (sorting). If these kinds of support are only formulated in very general terms, this is referred to as a logical access path. Logical access paths for primary keys can be broken down in accordance with sequential, tree-structured and scattered organizational forms. For secondary keys, which are of particular importance for relational database systems, access paths are created using inverted lists (index tables).

The design specification establishes which kinds of support should be set up for specific attributes. The entity type LOGICAL ACCESS PATH TYPE is created in Fig. B.II.24 to characterize the various types of support. The relationship between the attribute of a relation and an access path type then describes the logical access path. It is permissible

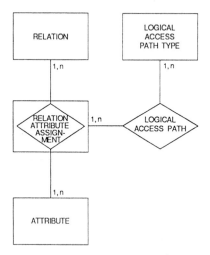

Fig. B.III.24: Logical access paths

for several access paths to be defined  for one attribute in a specific relation (that is for
one RELATION-ATTRIBUTE ASSIGNMENT).

The definition of access paths in the EDP concept is generated using global assumptions
about the number of tuples and the expected typical applications in a table. Once the
database is set up and real values concerning actual performance and actual operations
carried out on the database are available, then the access aids can be further
differentiated or altered in the implementation phase. By specifying logical access paths,
knowledge from the application-oriented design levels concerning database requirements
can be passed on to the implementation phase.


### B.III.3.5  Schema for a Database Management System

In the final step of the design specification the data structures are transferred into the
DDL of a specific database system, e. g. DB2, ORACLE or INGRES. A concrete database
system must be available to carry out this step. Since the relational model has a
mathematical formulation and the DML, and thus the integrity conditions formulated as
SQL statements, are standardized, the transfer of a relational database schema into the
DDL of a relational database system is a schematic process without any further degrees
of freedom.

If an enterprise employs several database systems in parallel, then the neutrally defined
relational schema can be translated into schemata oriented towards several database
management systems (DBMS). This is the case, for example, in software houses which
offer products in various database systems. Fig. B.III.25 indicates this situation by
defining the entity type DBMS, which contains the different database systems as entities.
A schema comprises the definition of relations which relate to a database management
system, including integrity conditions and access paths. This is shown in Fig. B.III.25 by
the creation of the complex object type SCHEMA. The assignment of this object type to a
database management system then generates its conceptual schema. This relationship
type can also be interpreted as the application of a special transformation rule to the
generally defined schema. For brevity, where reference is made in the subsequent
treatment to the schema, the complete contents will not be shown in a differentiated
representation, instead, the complex object SCHEMA will be represented by a box.

The relationship type CONCEPTUAL SCHEMA thus represents the entire schema with
reference to a data management system. It can be regarded quasi as a file, which can be
called up under the name of the schema.

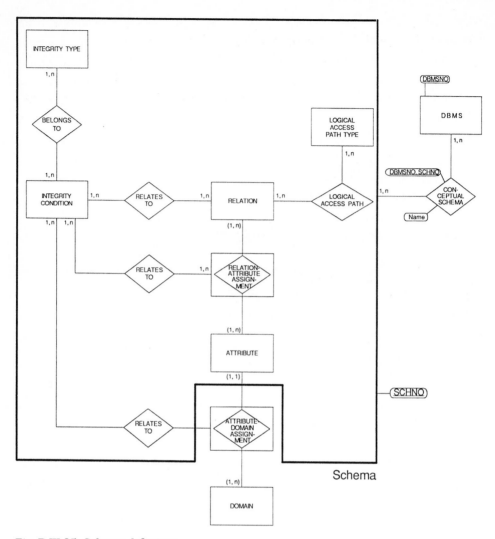

Fig. B.III.25: Schema definition

## B.III.4 Design Specification of the Control View

The incorporation of this section is shown in Fig. B.III.26. The control view of the design specification level is particularly important. Here, the relationships omitted in the separate consideration of the design views are reintegrated. In accordance with the principle of information hiding, whereby implementation issues should remain invisible to the user of an EDP component in order to relieve him of superfluous details and protect him from the multifarious effects of the information technology on the implementation, concrete EDP systems communicate with each other primarily at the level of the design specification of the control view.

The control view of the design specification is thus the central communication level of the ARIS architecture.

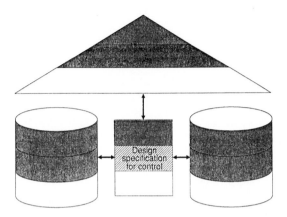

Fig. B.III.26: Incorporation of the design specification of the control view in ARIS

### B.III.4.1 Linking Module and Organization

In the context of the requirements definition, functions were assigned to the planning levels of an enterprise in accordance with their general responsibilities. In the context of the design specification, the concrete program objects (modules, panels and lists) are assigned to the organizational units down to the level of detail of the individual user. The assignment is effected by the definition of user authorizations. Examples of authorization types are permission to call up certain modules or input and output panels, or to be included in the distribution of listings. Fig. B.III.27 represents two ways of designing user authorizations. The individual authorization objects are referred to as program objects, which are the generalization of modules, panels and listings. If individual authorization functions are assigned to users in the form of an authorization matrix, then USER AUTHORIZATION constitutes a relationship type between the entity types AUTHORIZATION TYPE, USER and PROGRAM OBJECT. Users with identical authorization profiles are thereby described individually. This gives rise to costly and redundant management.

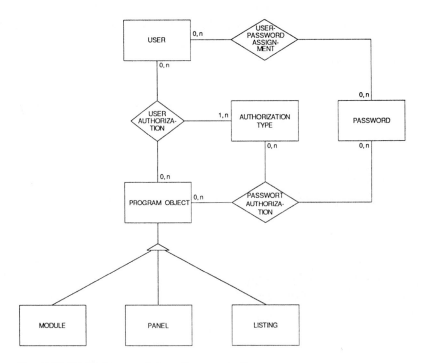

Fig. B.III.27: Linking module with organization

The second method presented avoids these redundancies. First, a password, or "PASSWORD AUTHORIZATION", is assigned to specific authorization profiles, which are then linked with individual users or groups of users via the relationship type "USER PASSWORD ASSIGNMENT". Using this indirect definition the redundancy of the specification is considerably reduced.

### B.III.4.2 Linking Module and Data

In the design specification of the function view modules are initially created without knowledge of a concrete data model, but only using global data definitions. Now, the modules and mini-specifications are linked with the data view of the design specification.

### B.III.4.2.1 External Schemata

From the data model view it makes no difference whether a "user" is a terminal user or a program module. The assignment of excerpts of the conceptual database schema to modules is thus defined in the same way as for the user.

An application or a user generally communicates not with the entire conceptual schema of a database, but only with excerpts thereof.

At the same time it may be useful to alter the name of the conceptual schema for specific applications. This can result, for example, if the independent development of an application has already incorporated definitions for attributes or relations in the design specification, which do not concur with those of the independently developed data model. The individual application or user's view of the logical database is defined by the external database schemata. These thus constitute the user interface with the conceptual schema. Individual instances can derive new relations from the relational schema, in that attributes or certain tuples are omitted from the basic relations, or basic relations are combined in accordance with certain criteria, or broken down into several relations. A way of expressing this is the definition of so-called (user) "views". Their general form (see e. g. *Mayr/Dittrich/Lockemann, Datenbankentwurf 1987, p. 537 ff.*) is as follows:

- define view (name of view),

- select (expression).

The structure resulting at the meta-level is represented in Fig. B.III.28. The entire conceptual schema, consisting of the relations, the attributes, and integrity conditions is represented by a complex object. The external schemata are linked with the conceptual schema via a grouping operation. A function or a user can thereby be assigned several external schemata, and conversely, an external schema several functions.

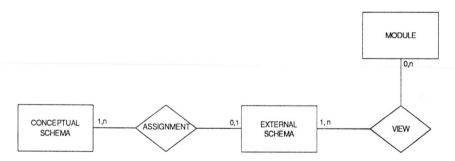

Fig. B.III.28: Linking module and database schema

It should be noted that this representation can only suggest the wide range of possibilities for transforming a conceptual schema into sub-schemata.

## B.III.4.2.2  Derivation of Control Structures

Control structures regulate process control, i. e. the sequence in which modules are
called up, for example. Process control is thereby oriented towards the data structures.
Basically, a program, or module, consists of data declaration, control logic and
instructions. The instructions are thus ultimately defined at the data element level, and
consequently correspond to the data element operations. In the context of structured
programming only a limited number of structures are permitted for process control:
- sequence,
- iteration,
- selection.

These control structures can be related to the data structures. A 1:1 relationship between
entity types corresponds to the sequence; a 1:n relationship to iteration, and the
specialization operation, in which information objects are broken down into sub-
concepts, to selection.

Fig. B.III.29 illustrates this with an example.

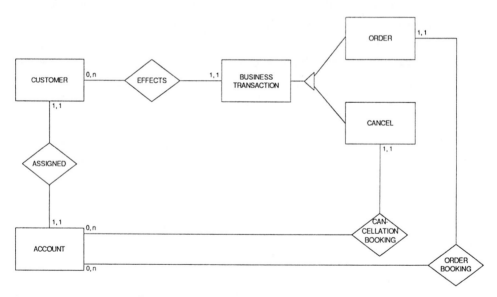

Fig. B.III.29: Example of the relationship between control structures and data structures

The information object CUSTOMER is always unambiguously assigned to one account
(1:1 relationship). A customer can participate in several business transactions. A
business transaction always relates to one customer. Business transactions are
specialized into orders and cancellations.

The different business transactions initiate different entry procedures. The resulting process control aspect is shown as a structogram in Fig. B.III.30. First, a customer record is read. Then the associated account is read. Given the cardinality of 1 which exists from the customer perspective, both processes constitute a sequence.

The business transactions, which from the customer viewpoint have a cardinality of n, are processed for the customer. This is represented as iteration.

Depending on the kind of business transaction diverse entries are made (selection on the basis of specialization).

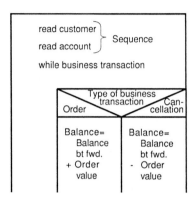

Fig. B.III.30: Example of control structures

The relationships between the cardinalities of the data structures and the control structure of the functional process are shown in Fig. B.III.31 as an information model. On the right side the structures MODULE and DATA ELEMENT OPERATORS are taken over from the function view.

On the left side the term INFORMATION OBJECT, introduced in the data modelling, is taken over along with its EDGE RELATIONSHIPS.

The entity type CONTROL STRUCTURE TYPE consists of the instances: sequence, iteration and selection. From the cardinalities of the data model, assignments to the control structures can be undertaken, which are represented here by the term "GENERATES". They can be taken over directly from the information objects EDGES or OPERATORS (in "is a" relationships). In order to shorten the representation, the entity type PROCESS STRUCTURE is introduced, which includes the terms INFORMATION OBJECT and EDGE as a complex object.

A module can be assigned specific information objects in the context of the data declaration. The incorporation of the individual data element operations in the process then occurs by creating a link between the process structure assigned to the module and the control structures thereby generated.

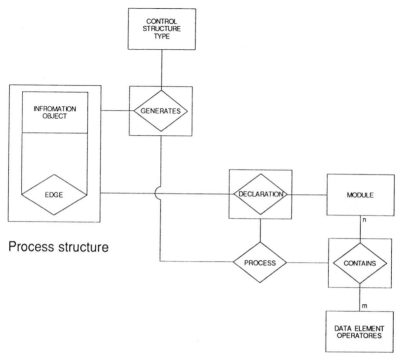

Fig. B.III.31: Data model and control structure relationships

### B.III.4.2.3 Database Transactions

The basis for changes in the database is the transaction concept. A transaction consists of a series of database operations which, from the application perspective, cannot be interrupted. This means that the consistency of the database from the application perspective is only ensured if the transaction is carried out in its entirety. If an error arises in the course of this process, the database is returned to its state before the transaction was started. This property of the transaction is referred to as atomicity: it has no effect on the database until it is successfully completed.

In addition to the **atomicity** or uninterruptability of a transaction, the transaction management must also ensure the **maintenance of consistency**, i. e. a transaction transfers the database from one consistent state to another consistent state.

Furthermore, the principle of **isolation** applies, i. e. no partial results may be passed on to other applications in the course of a transaction; as does the principle of **persistency** i. e. the effect of a successfully completed transaction is retained and can only be altered by new transactions.

The start and end of a transaction are indicated by terms (start of transaction, end of transaction). As many write and read instructions can be introduced within these brackets as is desired. The transaction is also the unit for data security measures (recovery).

From the program design perspective, a transaction can be interpreted as a module, or as a sequence of instructions within a module. In Fig. B.III.32 TRANSACTION is therefore presented as a specialization of the term MODULE. Since the design specification established that modules can be linked together in networks, these relationships are implicitly adopted.

A transaction combines several database operations, so that DATABASE OPERATION is a relationship type between the DB-OPERATION TYPE (e. g. read or write procedure), the associated TRANSACTION, and the INFORMATION OBJECT concerned.

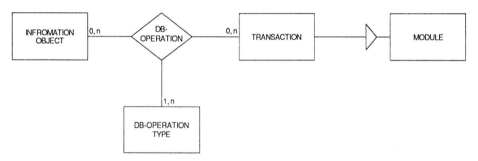

Fig. B.III.32: Transaction concept

## B.III.4.2.4  Trigger Control

Databases are not simply passive stores of enterprise data; components can be attached to them which react to certain application-specific events and initiate actions to alter the database. These components are referred to as triggers, and have already been introduced in the treatment of integrity conditions in the section on the design specification of the data view. With the help of triggers application functions can be activated, in which, for example, an inventory planning system constantly checks the stocks on hand of a part, so that the event "under-achievement of a minimum stock level" can initiate purchasing.

Basically, a trigger consists of a definition of the initiating event, the conditions which need to be checked whose fulfillment initiates certain actions. The actions are operations which alter data, that is, transactions.

Fig. B.III.33 represents the structure of the trigger concept. The entity type EVENT generates the link with the requirements definition level. An example of an event is the creation of a customer order. In addition to external events, there are also internal events which result from program applications, e. g. order confirmation. Certain times can also represent events, e. g. if certain actions always have to be carried out on the hour. Since time can also be defined as an entity type and is thus an information object, the term

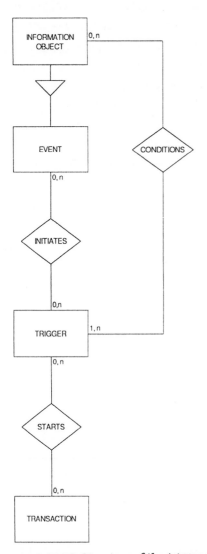

Fig. B.III.33: Structure of the trigger concept

event within the requirements definition covers the possible trigger initiators listed here. An event can thereby initiate several triggers, and a trigger can be initiated by several events.

Once a trigger has been initiated, various database states can be checked using the rules defined for the trigger. This is expressed by the relationship type CONDITIONS between TRIGGER and INFORMATION OBJECT.

If the condition applies, a trigger can initiate one or more transactions; conversely, a transaction can be initiated by various triggers. With respect to the example of checking stocks on hand, the initiating event could be time - as mentioned above - in that at regular intervals (e. g. hourly) the condition of whether stocks on hand have fallen below the minimum level is checked. An alternative event could be the recording of a withdrawal of the stocks concerned.

### B.III.4.3  Linking Organization and Data

Factors relating to users and institutional organizational units are considered under the organization view.

### B.III.4.3.1  Linking User and Data

The assignment of sub-schemata (external schemata) to users largely corresponds to the logic of assigning functions to data (see Fig. B.III.34).

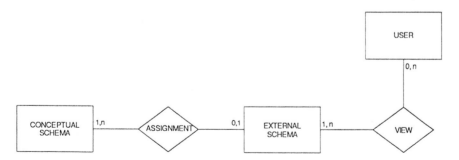

Fig. B.III.34: Linking user and data

A further important link between user and data are the authorizations which are assigned to a user with respect to data manipulation. Fig. B.III.35 gives an initial impression of the possibilities for defining access rights. Important access rights are reading, creating, updating and deleting. The objects in questions can be sub-divided. Thus, an entire relation can be regarded as an object, or a single attribute, a single tuple

| User | Database objects | | | | | Programs | |
|---|---|---|---|---|---|---|---|
| | Objects | | | | | | |
| | $O_1$ | $O_2$ | $O_3$. | | $O_n$ | $P_1$ | $P_2$ |
| $U_1$ | $R_1, R_2$ | | $R_3$ | | $R_i$ | $R_m$ | $R_n$ |
| $U_2$ | | $R_1$ | $R_2, R_3$ | | $R_1$ | $R_5, R_6$ | ... |
| $U_3$ | | $R_2, R_3$ | $R_2$ | | | | |
| . | | | | | | | |
| . | | | | | | | |
| . | | | | | | | |
| $U_m$ | $R_1, R_2$ | $R_i$ | $R_1$ | | $R_i, R_k$ | $R_n$ | $R_s$ |

$U_i$   $1 \leq i \leq m$ set of users
$O_i$   $1 \leq i \leq n$ set of objects in DB
$R_i$   $1 \leq i \leq s$ set of access rights
$P_i$   $1 \leq i \leq l$ set of access programs

Fig. B.III.35: User authorization table

from: *Reuter, Sicherheits- und Integritätsbedingungen 1987, p. 352*

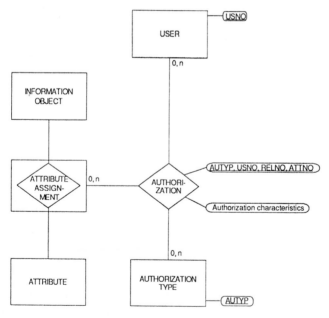

Fig. B.III.36: User authorizations

or a set of tuples. Selection criteria can also be logical links to the data contents, for example, if a department head is only allowed to read from the employee records relating to employees in his department. In another example from the same application area, it can be specified that an employee from the personnel department is only allowed to read data records for employees whose salary is below some fixed level.

This case is represented in Fig. B.III.36 as a relationship type between the relation USER and the relation ATTRIBUTE ASSIGNMENT. The relationship type thus contains the definition of a certain type of concrete authorization. In addition to the direct relationship

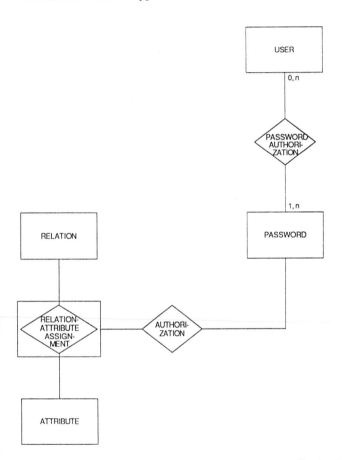

Fig. B.III.37: Data structure for representing user authorizations

between USER and the RELATION - ATTRIBUTE ASSIGNMENT, an indirect relationship can also be generated, such as that offered by the database system ADABAS, in which authorizations are first assigned to specific passwords and these then to specific users.

This makes non-redundant representation possible, since two users who have the same authorization profile also obtain the same password. The information model is presented in Fig. B.III.37.

The protection mechanism can be formulated using a tabular representation. All relevant queries to the database must be checked using the table. A special implementation form is offered by the relational database system INGRES. Here, the authorization rules are formulated as so-called range-conditions, which are then, on execution of the query, amalgamated into **one** DML instruction using the query formulation and thus processed in the same syntax. A self-explanatory example is given in Fig. B.III.38.

Verbal                                    In the DML QUEL from Ingres

Formulation of the access conditions

Departmental head Müller            RANGE OF X IS EMPLOYEE
may access all records for           RESTRICT
employees in his department          ACCESS FOR
A43                                  'MUELLER' TO EMPLOYEE
                                     WHERE X.DEPT.MEMB.='A43'

Formulation of the query:

Search for names of                  RANGE OF X IS EMPLOYEE
all employees who earn               RETRIEVE INTO LIST (X.NAME)
more than 50,000 DM                  WHERE WAGE > 50,000

Consolidated query

                                     RANGE OF X IS EMPLOYEE
                                     RETRIEVE INTO LIST (X.NAME)
                                     WHERE X.WAGE < 50,000
                                     AND
                                     X.DEPT.MEMB.='A43'

Fig. B.III.38: User authorizations in QUEL

from: *Reuter, Sicherheits- und Integritätsbedingungen 1987, pp. 361, 362*

## B.III.4.3.2 Linking Organizational Units and Data: Distributed Databases

Thus far, it has been assumed that the database is, at least logically, localized in one place. In the context of the discussion of distributed databases, excerpts from the schema are distributed to various computer nodes. These excerpts can be handled by diverse data management systems, although they communicate with each other. The database system is thus divided into two levels: first, there are components which manage the local data records of one node, then there are components which look after the coordination between the local data records.

The reasons for using distributed databases are the increased availability of the entire system, improved up-to-dateness, lower costs and increased flexibility (see *Nerreter, Zur funktionalen Architektur von verteilten Datenbanken 1983, p. 2 f.; Jablonski, Datenverwaltung in verteilten Systemen 1990, p. 5*).

The characteristics of a distributed database are summarized by Date in 12 rules, whereby rule 0 is the "fundamental principle of a distributed database" (see *Date, Twelve Rules For Distributed Database Systems 1987*). The rules are:

Rule 0:          Fundamental principle.

                 A distributed database must appear to the user as undistributed, i. e. as a centralized database.

                 This rule justifies the maintenance of the uniformly defined integrity conditions and access authorizations, since the fundamental schema is not affected by the data distribution.

Rule 1:          Local autonomy.

                 Each node should manage the local data assigned to it locally, i. e. data security, data integrity and data storage should be monitored locally. This ensures that purely local operations do not involve any disadvantage associated with the distributed system.

Rule 2:          No reliance on a central site.

This means that each location enjoys "equal rights". The subordination to a central system would immediately impair the entire system were the latter to break down.

Rule 3:          Continuous operation.

The system should not need to be interrupted by the switching on or off of any locations.

Rule 4:          Local independence.

The user should not be required to know the location at which data are stored.

Rule 5:          Fragmentation independence.

Relations can be broken down into fragments in order to improve the efficiency of the system. The user can nevertheless behave as if the data record (relation) has not been segmented.

Rule 6:          Replication independence.

The same data can be allocated as copies to several locations. The user does not need to be aware of the existence of copies.

Rule 7:          Distributed query processing.

Optimizers can be used for distributed query processing.

Rule 8:          Distributed transaction management.

In a distributed system every individual transaction can involve update processes at other locations. If a transaction is not completed the update must be rescinded.

Rule 9:            Hardware independence.

The database management system should operate on diverse hardware systems.


Rule 10:           Operating system independence.

The database management system should be capable of running on diverse operating systems.


Rule 11:           Network independence.

The database management system should support various networks.


Rule 12:           Database management system independence.

A distributed database system should also be possible using diverse local database management systems, e. g. by creating gateways as bridges between diverse databases.

The information model in Fig. B.III.39 is developed taking these properties into account. In the process reference is made to the terms introduced in the design specification of the organization view (expressed in the network topology) and the data view (expressed in the relational schema).

A formulation of data distribution with the help of Wedekind's object type method has been developed by Jablonski (see *Jablonski, Datenverwaltung in verteilten Systemen 1990, p. 198*); it will be partially followed in the discussion below.

The fragmentation property means that a relation can be segmented horizontally and/or vertically. Each fragment is then assigned the key of the base relation. The fragments can overlap each other (see Fig. B.III.40).

The fragments created are represented in Fig. B.III.39 by the entity type SEGMENT. Each segment is then assigned unambiguously to one relation. If a segment is assigned to a particular computer node and database management system this allocated data segment

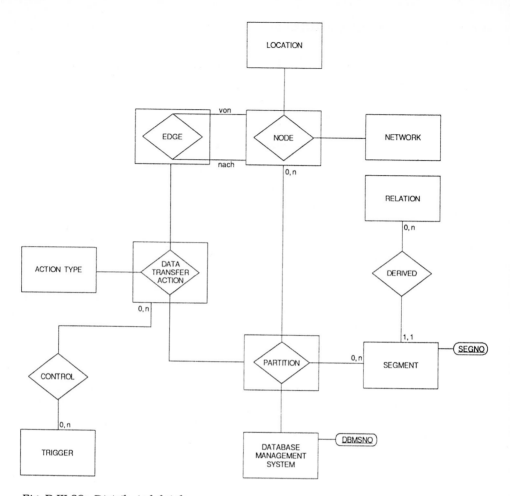

Fig. B.III.39: Distributed databases

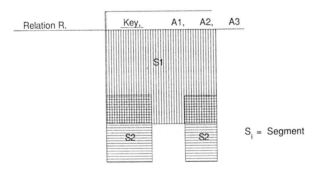

Fig. B.III.40: Segmenting a relation

is referred to as a PARTITION (see *Jablonski, Datenverwaltung in verteilten Systemen 1990, p.193*).

An important component of the description of data distribution is establishing the rules governing the execution of a distributed data processing action. Local data processing tasks can generate data which are also offered to other nodes. Thus, data exchanges between the partitions of various nodes occur. Nodes which are possible recipients then need to take up the data provided in a takeover procedure.

The entire process of this action is effected in two phases: the offer phase and the acceptance up phase, see Fig. B.III.41 for a CIM example.

**Sub-application CAP**                                        **Sub-application CAM**

Fig. B.III.41: Example of a distributed data processing action
after: *Jablonski, Datenverwaltung in verteilten Systemen 1990, p. 148*

The sub-application CAP (Computer Aided Planning) generates a production order $PO_{new}$, which is taken up in the relation "production order" (step 1). The sub-application CAP is aware that the sub-application CAM has an interest in this data amendment. The CAP control area therefore generates an update message for the new data (step 2), and offers this to the CAM control area by placing it in the intermediate buffer area (step 3). The sub-application CAM takes these data out of the intermediate buffer (step 4), processes them in accordance with its rules (step 5), and places them in the corresponding relation of its node (step 6).

Different procedures can be established for the two phases offer and acceptance. In the case of a direct offer, the updates in the primary application are immediately offered to the secondary application. In the case of an indirect offer, however, the data amendments in the primary area are only offered to the secondary application once an event arises.

In the case of synchronous acceptance of modification data, the data placed in the buffer are removed immediately; in the case of asynchronous acceptance they are only called up when an event arises.

The two phases of offer and acceptance are represented in Fig. B.III.39 by the entity type ACTION TYPE. The relationship type DATA TRANSFER ACTION is thus indicated by the combination of the entity types ACTION TYPE (offer or take-up), the PARTITION involved from the sender and the recipient (EDGE).

The strategy employed (direct or indirect, synchronous or asynchronous) is generated by the assignment of certain triggers. The triggers establish those events to which the system should react. As soon as an event occurs the trigger conditions are checked. If they apply, the trigger "fires" and initiates the corresponding action. Actions are the placing of data in the buffer area from the offer viewpoint, and the processing of data from the buffer area from the acceptance viewpoint.

### B.III.4.4 Linking Module, Organization and Data (Distributed Data Processing)

Distributed databases simply consider the relationship between the data and the organization views. If the function view is added to this analysis, then one speaks of distributed data **processing**. Strictly speaking, the border with distributed data processing has already been crossed by the consideration of trigger concepts, since they assign the processing functions of database systems. For this reason, these are also referred to as active database systems.

At this stage the modules are also assigned to the nodes of a computer network. Modules represent the processing steps of an application system. Thus, they can also have events as results which trip data transfer triggers in a distributed database system. Fig. B.III.42 extends the concept of the distributed database to include the assignment of the function view.

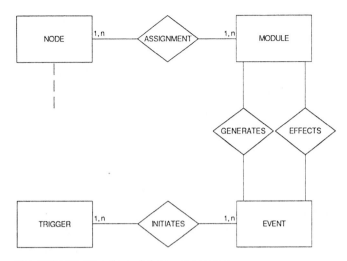

Fig. B.III.42: Distributed data processing

## B.IV  Design of the Implementation Description

In the implementation phase the existing design specification is transformed into a workable system. In this process the specifications are adapted to the concrete device and software requirements. Since the components of an information system at this stage are found at the level of concrete hardware and software products, there is close dependence on information technology developments.

The relationships between the design specification and the implementation are closer than those between the requirements definition and the design specification. This is a result of the fact that the design and implementation phases often overlap. In a concrete project, parts of the system can already be implemented while the design specification is still being developed for other parts. Also, performance problems often only become visible in the course of implementation, and can then necessitate amendments to the design specification.

In the transformation of units of the design specification into physical units, new objects emerge which can be represented by their own terms in the information model.

The strong parallels between the results of the design specification and the implementation phase highlight the close interdependence of the two levels. Consequently, automated transformation procedures incorporating optimization possibilities can increasingly be employed.

Given the more limited problem issues associated with this phase as compared with the earlier ones, which gives rise to a more mechanistic transformation, the implementation is not treated in as much detail as the other levels.

### B.IV.1 Implementation Description of the Function View

The incorporation of this section is shown in Fig. B.IV.01.

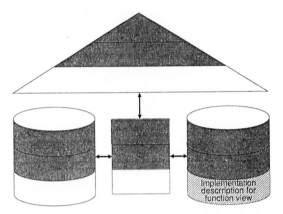

Fig. B.IV.01: Incorporation of the implementation description of the function view in ARIS

On the basis of the module specifications developed in the design specification, e. g. in pseudo code, the concrete executable program is developed in the course of the implementation. This is created in a programming language (e. g. COBOL, FORTRAN, PASCAL, C, PROLOG). If the initial specifications already exist in sufficient detail for them to be translated into program code using a generator, then the resulting source code module is a relationship between the module description of the design specification, the programming language and the translation tool used (see Fig. B.IV.02). If the programming is carried out entirely by (human) programmers, then the reference to the tool used is eliminated.

The source code modules can be placed in a program library. The program library lists all existing programs or modules, and its use increases decisively the re-use of modules. Program libraries can already be employed at the design specification level for module specifications, for this reason, the relationship to the module term of the design specification is also included in Fig. B.IV.02.

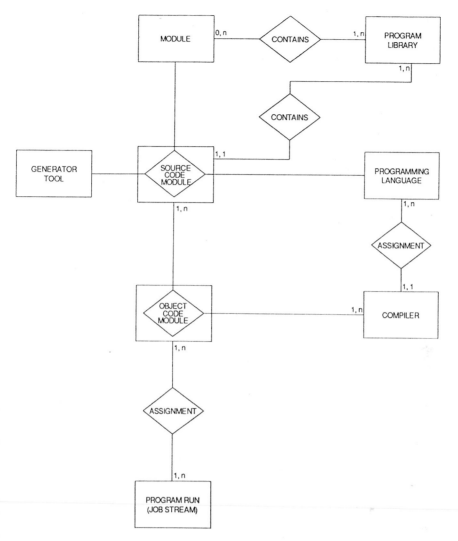

Fig. B.IV.02: Module transformation into source code

A source code module is translated into the executable object code module with the help of a compiler. Several compilers can exist for each programming language, e. g. for different hardware systems. Correspondingly, several object code modules can be derived from one source code module.

For the complete handling of a task several modules are generally required, which together compose a program. The term program can be regarded as a higher level module and therefore does not require an independent term.

Several programs can be combined into a job stream. A typical example is the processing of batch runs during computer centre's night shift. Here, it is necessary to ensure that the programs form a self-contained sequence, i. e., the data updates carried out by one program must be completed before the next program starts. A data security concept relating to the job stream is also important. Whereas the design of such a data security concept still relates to the implementation level, and could thus be regarded as part of the build-time version, the implementation of the security measures is explicitly a task of the run-time approach.

## B.IV.2 Implementation Description of the Organization View

The incorporation of this section is shown in Fig. B.IV.03.

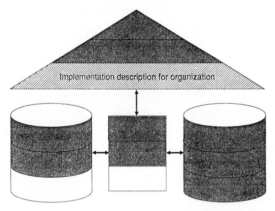

Fig. B.IV:03: Incorporation of the implementation description of the organization view in ARIS

The starting point for the implementation is the network topology, which is represented in the upper part of Fig. B.IV.04 as an information model. The networks and nodes defined in the design specification can be physically implemented in a form which deviates from their logical definition. Consequently, the terms from the requirements definiton are preceded by an L. if they exist in the same form at the physical level. Correspondingly, the terms at the implementation level are indicated by the prefix PH. This should make clear that the logically defined components are now transformed into physical units. Fig. B.IV.05 presents an example of a heterogeneous network configuration.

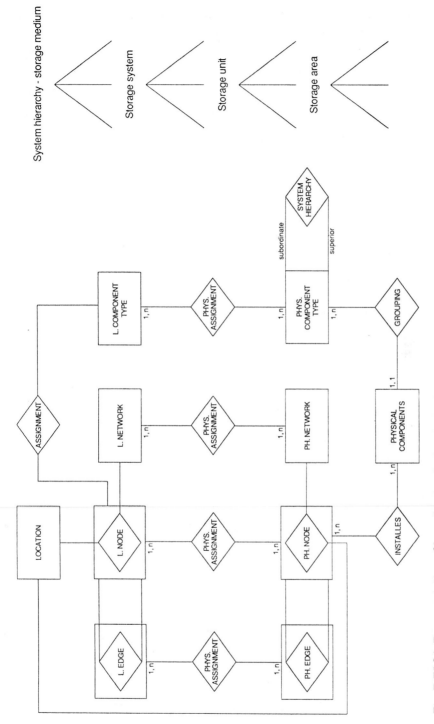

Fig. B.IV.04: Representation of logical networks by physical networks

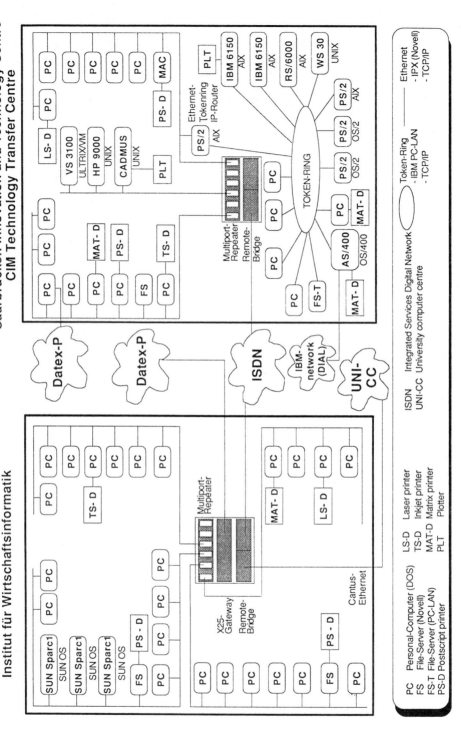

Fig. B.IV.05: Example of a heterogeneous network architecture

from: *Houy/Klein, Die Vernetzungsstrategie des Instituts für Wirtschaftsin-*

A specific network protocol (e. g. ETHERNET, SNA, or TCP/IP) is represented in the implementation by a physical network. The physical network is thus characterized by its concrete transfer medium, e. g., coaxial cable, fibre optic cable, or double core telephone cable. An n:m relationship can exist between the entity type L.NETWORK (logical network) and the entity type PH.NETWORK (physical network). Several logical networks can be represented by one physical network, and one logically unified network can be realized by several physical networks which can be switched together.

Corresponding to the data structure of the design specification, a physical network node is designed as a link between the physical network PH.NETWORK to which it belongs, and a location description LOCATION. The location definition is thus taken over from the design specification, whereby its instances can be extended. An n:m relationship also exists between the terms physical node (PH.NODE) and the logical node (L.NODE), since from the perspective of the design specification several physical nodes can exist at one logical node. Conversely, physical nodes can exist which have no direct relationship to a logical node at the design specification level, e. g. if the physical node only possesses technical amplification functions, without application devices or application functions being assigned to it.
The physical network is defined by physical nodes and physical edges.

An n:m relationship is also generated between the terms logical edge (L.EDGE) and physical edge (PH.EDGE).
Of course, it should be noted that for the purposes of designing an information model these relationships are not absolutely essential. It may suffice simply to manage the links between the logical network and the physical network, and where necessary between sub-sets of the logical and physical nodes, whereas the physical edge definitions are simply needed in the implementation environment and the relationship to the logical edges does not need to be generated.

The device level, that is the computer components, are characterized by the term PHYSICAL COMPONENT TYPE. This is linked with the design specification level by an assignment relationship to the entity type L.COMPONENT TYPE. For example, a specific family of devices with manufacturer and type specifications can be assigned to the storage system term at the logical level. The hierarchical link between the upper system and the interlocking sub-systems are represented by the relationship type SYSTEM HIERARCHY. In this way, complex computer systems or storage systems can be broken down into a kind of bill of materials structure. The individual physical components of a

196

special type are represented by the entity type PHYSICAL COMPONENTS. In addition to the grouping into specific component types, the assignment to the location, expressed by the physical node of a network, is also generated here. A physical node can be linked with several physical components of a computer system. Conversely, a physical computer component can also be linked up with several networks and hence several physical nodes.

System software components can be regarded in the same way as the hardware oriented components. For instance, in addition to control computers, the corresponding control software is used for network control. This largely analogous description is not pursued further here. This implies the assumption that the system software is part of the hardware components.

The issues relating to the implementation of user authorizations are also not considered further here. This amounts to the assumption that the tables and triggers established at the requirements definition and the design specification levels can be physically implemented without further design considerations.

### B.IV.3 Implementation Description of the Data View

The implementation description of the data view is incorporated in Fig. B.IV.06.

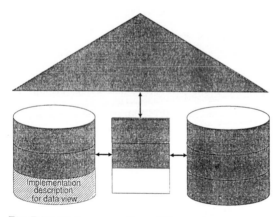

Fig. B.IV.06: Incorporation of the implementation description of the data view in ARIS

## B.VI.3.1. Storage

The starting point is the design specification of the data view, which includes the conceptual database schema, that is the definition of relations, attributes and integrity conditions. Logical access paths to certain attribute assignments are also defined there on the basis of rough estimates of the frequency of applications or queries.

In the implementation context, the conceptual schema is represented as an internal schema. This means that the internal schema describes the same portion of reality as the conceptual schema. No semantics are added. Indeed, the internal schema can be derived from the conceptual schema without any knowledge of the semantic environment.

The structuring of the internal schema is the task of the database administrator. He creates efficient physical data structures given the EDP techniques available. In doing this he must take into account the utilization profile of the various applications with respect to their data, their volume and their required response times. These details require no knowledge of the semantic references (contents) of the applications.

The independence of the implementation layer is also supported by the use of independent terms, which again find parallels at the logical level of the design specification (see Fig. B.IV.07). For instance, the terms RELATION and ATTRIBUTE are assigned to the implementation terms RECORD and FIELD. The term RECORD does not describe the individual instances (or tuples) but the type of record, which is always indicated by a fixed attribute combination. A storage page can thus include various record types. The aim of the optimization carried out by the database administrator is to place record types which are frequently required together in physical proximity.

The levels of the design specification can be distinguished from the implementation levels in that, as compared with the attributes of the relational schema, the fields can take on a different sequence, their names can be altered, data condensed, or concrete field formats generated. Furthermore, virtual fields can be agreed, i. e. transformation rules can be defined for fields if their contents consist of the amalgamation of other fields (e. g. field totals).

Differences can arise with respect to relations or records if relations are sub-divided into several records, or if several relations are combined into a single physical record.

The integrity and consistency conditions defined at the design specification level are made concrete at the physical level by procedural constructs.

198

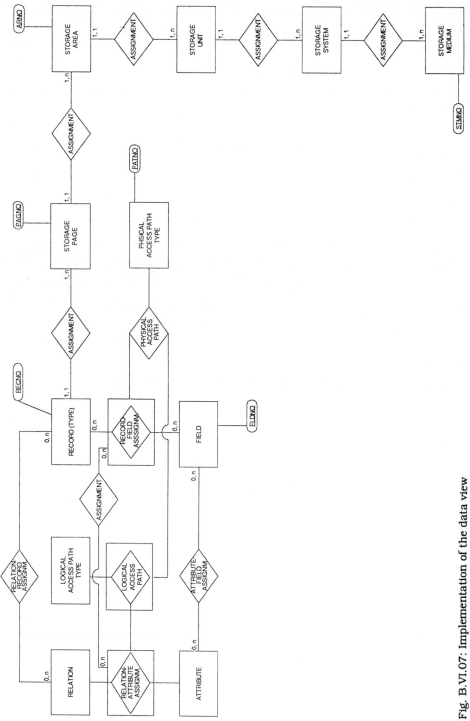

Fig. B.VI.07: Implementation of the data view

Further extensions at the implementation level are the assignment of concrete physical access methods to the logical access paths, or the definition of additional physical access paths.

In addition to the terms RECORD and FIELD which largely correspond to the design specification, the sub-divisions STORAGE PAGE and STORAGE AREA are introduced at the physical level in Fig. B.IV.07, which form additional organizational elements for optimizing the storage assignment structures. These general elements provide a basis for data access to external stores (in that entire pages are always transported), and for the assignment to physical storage units.

The optimization possibilities with respect to storage pages and storage areas are obvious from plausibility considerations. Thus, a storage access to several records which are assigned to the same page is more efficient than to records which are distributed over different storage pages. Similarly, the access to storage pages which are in close numerical order is more efficient than to widely distributed storage pages.

The data storage description language (DSDL) is used for referencing between the internal and external model, as well as for implementing storage assignment structures.

The physical access paths are represented by concrete index tables, chains or hash functions.

The close parallels with the conceptual schema are obvious. In the case of complete conformity between the descriptions, the assignments merely consist of notational references. Given the independent optimization goals, however, considerable alterations arise between the logical and physical data descriptions. The physical access paths are defined at the level of the record-field assignment. They are either concrete versions of the logical access paths from the design specification, or they are newly created at the implementation level on the basis of detailed knowledge of performance criteria.

The definition of the physical data structures level follows essentially from the design objective of data independence. Device and system software changes should only affect the implementation level, but not the conceptual database schema. For this reason, several internal database schemata can exist over time for a single conceptual database schema. Conversely, a conceptual database schema can be altered without changing the physical schema. Thus, in general, an n:m relationship exists between the logical and the internal schema (see Fig. B.IV.08).

200

Fig. B.IV.08: Conceptual and internal schema

## B.IV.3.2 Storage Assignment

The physical storage media are represented by the hierarchy storage medium, storage system, and storage unit (see Fig. B.IV.06). The entity type STORAGE MEDIUM describes the various types of storage , such as hard disk storage, mountable disks, floppy disks or magnetic tape. A STORAGE SYSTEM comprises a uniform group of concrete storage units within a storage medium, e. g. a storage system might be a disk layout for a certain type of disk with various disk drives. The assignment of the physical storage structures to the physical storage units is generated via storage areas.

## B.IV.4 Implementation Description of the Control View

This section is incorporated in Fig. B.IV.09. In the control view the implemented components are linked with each other.

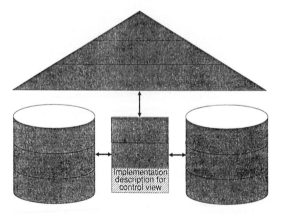

Fig. B.IV:09: Incorporating the implementation of the control view in ARIS

This means, for example, that the physical files required, and other resources in terms of computer power and storage, are assigned to a concrete job stream. This is referred to here as reservation. The requirements on the reserved components are thereby derived from the assignments established in the context of the control view of the requirements definition. In general, the views also communicate with each other at the design specification level. The link with the implementation phase is thus represented only in general terms in Fig. B.IV.10

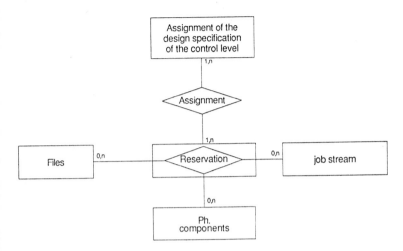

Fig. B.IV.10: Control view of the implemented components

**B.V The ARIS Information Model**

The information model developed in the book is summarized in the fold-out Fig. B.V.

# References:

Aderibigde, A., Eide, C., Stewart, J. A.: *Computer-Aided Software Engineering 1990*
Computer-Aided Software Engineering (CASE) Open Road. Discussion paper of the
Open Software Foundation (OSF), Cambridge 1990.

Association for Computing Machinery (ACM) (ed.): *Objektorientierte Programmierung 1990*
Communications of the ACM. Vol. 33 (1990), No. 9.

Aue, D., Baresch, M., Keller, G.: *URMEL 1990*
URMEL: Ein Unternehmensmodellierungsansatz. Saarbrücken 1990.
(Veröffentlichungen des Instituts für Wirtschaftsinformatik, no. 71, ed.: A.-W.
Scheer).

Balzert, H. (Ed.): *CASE: Systeme und Werkzeuge 1990*
CASE: Systeme und Werkzeuge. 2nd ed., Mannheim-Vienna Zurich 1990.

Balzert, H.: *Die Entwicklung von Software-Systemen 1982*
Die Entwicklung von Software-Systemen (Prinzipien, Methoden, Sprachen,
Werkzeuge). Mannheim-Vienna-Zurich 1982.

Barker, R.: *CASE*Method 1990*
CASE*Method: tasks and deliverables. Wokingham-Reading-Menlo Park-et al. 1990.

Baumgarten, B.: *Petri-Netze 1990*
Petri-Netze: Grundlagen und Anwendungen. Mannheim-Vienna Zurich 1990.

Blaser, A., Jarke, M., Lehmann, H., et al.: *Datenbanksprachen und Datenbankbenutzung
1987*
Datenbanksprachen und Datenbankbenutzung. In: Lockemann, P. C., Schmidt, J.
W. (eds.): Datenbank-Handbuch. Berlin-Heidelberg-New York-et al. 1987, pp. 559 -
667.

Brenner, W.: *Entwurf betrieblicher Datenelemente 1988*
Entwurf betrieblicher Datenelemente - Ein Weg zur Integration von
Informationssystemen. Berlin-Heidelberg-New York et al. 1988.

Breuker, J., Wielinga, B., van Someren, M., et al.: *Model Driven Knowledge Acquisition 1987*

Model Driven Knowledge Acquisition: Interpretation Models, Esprit Project P1098, Deliverable D1 (task A1). University of Amsterdam and SLT Ltd. 1987.


Brodie, M. L., Ridjanovic, D., Silva, E. O.: *Framework for Information Systems 1983*

On a Framework for Information systems Design Methodologies. In: Olle, T. W., Sol, H. G., Tully, C. J. (eds.): Information Systems Design Methodologies: A Feature Analysis. Proceedings of the IFIP WG 8.1 Working Conference on Feature Analysis of Information Systems Design Methodologies, York, U.K., 5-7 July, 1983, Amsterdam-New York-Oxford-et al. 1983, pp. 231 - 242.


Busch, R.: *Entwurf eines Systems zur integrierten Fertigung 1989*

Entwurf eines Systems zur integrierten Fertigung (CIM) mit Petri-Netzen. In: Zeitschrift für Betriebswirtschaft, 59 (1989), no. 8, pp. 822 - 838.


Chen, P. P.: *Entity-Relationship Model 1976*

The Entity-Relationship Model (Towards an Unified View of Data). ACM Transactions on Database-Systems, no. 1 (1976), pp. 9 - 36.


Date, C. J.: *Relational Database 1986*

Relational Database: Selected Writings. Reading-Menlo Park-Don Mills- et al. 1986.


Date, C. J.: *Twelve Rules For Distributed Databasesystem 1987*

Twelve Rules For Distributed Databasesystem. In: Computerworld, June 1987.


Davis, G. B., Olson, M.: *Management Information Systems 1984*

Management Information Systems (Conceptual Foundations, Structure, and Development). New York 1984.


Dittrich, K. R.: *Stand und Tendenzen der "nachrelationalen" Datenbanktechnologie 1990*

Objektorientiert, aktiv, erweiterbar: Stand und Tendenzen der "nachrelationalen" Datenbanktechnologie. In: Scheer, A.-W. (ed.): Praxis relationaler Datenbanken. Saarbrücken 1990, pp. 1 - 21.


Elmaghraby, S. E.: *Activity networks 1977*

Activity networks: project planning and control by network models. New York-et al. 1977.

ESPRIT Consortium AMICE (ed.): *Open System Architecture 1989*

Open System Architecture for CIM. In: Research Reports ESPRIT, Project 688, AMICE, Vol. 1, Berlin-Heidelberg-New York-et al. 1989.


Falkenberg, E., Nijssen, G. M., Adams, A., et al.: *Feature Analysis 1983*

Feature Analysis of ACM/PCM, CIAM, ISAC and NIAM. In: Olle, T. W., Sol, H. G., Tully, C. J. (eds.): Information Systems Design Methodologies: A Feature Analysis. Proceedings of the IFIP WG 8.1 Working Conference on Feature Analysis of Information Systems Design Methodologies, York, U.K., 5-7 July, 1983, Amsterdam-New York-Oxford-et al. 1983, pp. 169 - 190.


Ferstl, O. K., Sinz, E. J.: *Objektmodellierung betrieblicher Informationssysteme 1990*

Objektmodellierung betrieblicher Informationssysteme im Semantischen Objektmodell (SOM). In: Wirtschaftsinformatik. 32 (1990), no. 6, pp. 567 - 581.


Fimmler, G., Groditzki, G.: *IBM Enterprise Business Process Reference Model 1990*

IBM Enterprise Business Process Reference Model. Draft version 1.0, Munich 1990.


Fisher, D. T.: *Produktivität durch Information Engineering 1990*

Produktivität durch Information Engineering. Braunschweig-Wiesbaden 1990.


Fosdick, H.: *Ten Steps To AD/Cycle 1990*

Ten Steps To AD/Cycle. In: Datamation. December 1, 1990, pp. 59 - 64.


Gabriel, R.: *Software Engineering 1990*

Software Engineering. In: Kurbel, K., Strunz, H. (eds.): Handbuch Wirtschaftsinformatik. Stuttgart 1990, pp. 257 - 273.


Gutenberg, E.: *Die Produktion 1983*

Grundlagen der Betriebswirtschaftslehre. Vol. 1: Die Produktion. 24th ed., Berlin-Heidelberg-New York 1983.


Gutzwiller, T., Österle, H.: *Referenz-Meta-Modell Analyse 1990*

CC RIM, Referenz-Meta-Modell Analyse. Report No.: IM2000/CCRIM/2, version 2.0, Institut für Wirtschaftsinformatik, Hochschule St. Gallen, January 15, 1990.

Gutzwiller, T., Österle, H.: *Referenzbeispiel Analyse 1990*

CC RIM, Referenzbeispiel Analyse. Report No.: IM2000/CCRIM/3, version 2.0, Institut für Wirtschaftsinformatik, Hochschule St. Gallen, January 15, 1990.


Härder, T.: *Grenzen und Erweiterungsmöglichkeiten relationaler Datenbanksysteme 1989*

Grenzen und Erweiterungsmöglichkeiten relationaler Datenbanksysteme für Nicht-Standard-Anwendungen. In: Scheer, A.-W. (Ed.): Praxis relationaler Datenbanken. Saarbrücken 1989, pp. 1 - 25.


Härder, T.: *Non-Standard-Datenbanksysteme 1990*

Non-Standard-Datenbanksysteme - Anforderungen, Datenmodell- und Architekturkonzepte. In: Scheer, A.-W. (ed.): Praxis relationaler Datenbanken. Saarbrücken 1990, pp. 23 - 58.


Hazzah, A.: *Application development 1990*

Rosetta Stone for Developers? - Model built by IBM and partners charts new course for application development. In: Software Magazine, July 1990, pp. 87 - 96.


Heilmann, H.: *Organisationsinformationssystem 1989*

Entwurfsentscheidungen bei der Gestaltung eines Organisationsinformationssystems. In: Kurbel, K., Mertens, P., Scheer, A.-W. (eds.): Interaktive betriebswirtschaftliche Informations- und Kommunikationssysteme. Berlin-New York 1989, pp. 315 - 328.


Heinrich, L. J., Burgholzer, P.: *Systemplanung I 1989*

Systemplanung: die Planung und Realisierung von Informations- und Kommunikationssystemen. Vol. 1: Der Prozeß der Großprojektierung, der Feinprojektierung und der Implementierung. 4th ed., Munich-Vienna 1986.


Heinrich, L. J., Burgholzer, P.: *Systemplanung II 1986*

Systemplanung: die Planung und Realisierung von Informations- und Kommunikationssystemen. Vol. 2: Der Prozeß der Großprojektierung, der Feinprojektierung und der Implementierung. 2nd ed., Munich-Vienna 1986


Heinrich, L. J., Roithmayr F.: *Wirtschaftsinformatik - Lexikon 1989*

Wirtschaftsinformatik - Lexikon. 3rd revised and extended ed., Munich-Vienna 1989.

Hildebrand, K.: *Software Tools 1990*

Software Tools: Auomatisierung im Software Engineering - Eine umfassende Darstellung der Einsatzmöglichkeiten von Software-Entwicklungswerkzeugen. Berlin-Heidelberg-New York-et al. 1990.


Houy, C., Klein, J.: *Die Vernetzungsstrategie des Instituts für Wirtschaftsinformatik 1991*

Die Vernetzungsstrategie des Instituts für Wirtschaftsinformatik - Migration vom PC-Netzwerk zum Wide Area Network. Saarbrücken 1991 (Veröffentlichungen des Instituts für Wirtschaftsinformatik, no. 76, ed.: A.-W. Scheer).


Hoyer, R., Kölzer, G.: *Gestaltung von Büroinformationsssystemen 1988*

Rechnergestützte Planung und Gestaltung von Büroinformations- und - kommunikationssystemen. Berlin 1988.


Hutchinson, Marian, Shephard: *Local Area Networks 1985*

Local Area Networks: An Advanced Course, Lecture Notes in Computer Science. Berlin-Heidelberg-New York 1985.


IBM (ed.): *DevelopMate 1989*

DevelopMate - General Information. Version 1, Release 1, GC26-4641-O, 1989


IBM (ed.): *Repository Manager/MVS 1989*

Repository Manager/MVS - General Information. Version 1, Release 1, GC26-4608-O, 1989


Jablonski, S.: *Datenverwaltung in verteilten Systemen 1990*

Datenverwaltung in verteilten Systemen: Grundlagen und Lösungskonzepte. Berlin-Heidelberg-New York-et al. 1990.


Jarke, M., Jeusfeld, M., Rose, T.: *A Software Process Data Model 1990*

A Software Process Data Model for Knowledge Engineering in Information Systems. In: Information Systems, Vol. 15 (1990), no. 1, pp. 85 - 116.


Jorysz, H. R., Vernadat F. B.: *CIM-OSA Part 1: total enterprise modelling and function view 1990*

CIM-OSA Part 1: total enterprise modelling and function view. In: International Journal of Computer Integrated Manufacturing, 3 (1990), no. 3 and 4, pp. 144 - 156.

Jorysz, H. R., Vernadat, F. B.: *CIM-OSA Part 2: information view 1990*
CIM-OSA Part 2: information view. In: International Journal of Computer Integrated Manufacturing, 3 (1990), no. 3 and 4, pp. 157 - 167.

Jost, W., Keller, G., Scheer, A.-W.: *Konzeption eines DV-Tools im Rahmen der CIM-Planung 1991*
Konzeption eines DV-Tools im Rahmen der CIM-Planung: Gestaltung unternehmensspezifischer Funktions- und Informationsarchitekturen. In: Zeitschrift für Betriebswirtschaft, 61 (1991), no. 1, pp. 33 - 64.

Kargl, H.: *Fachentwurf für DV-Anwendungssysteme 1989*
Fachentwurf für DV-Anwendungssysteme. Munich-Vienna 1989.

Kelting, E. H.: *AD/Cycle 1990*
IBM's Vision zur Lösung der Anwendungsentwicklungsprobleme: AD/Cycle. In: Information Management, 5 (1990), no. 2, pp. 40 - 43.

Knappe, T., Suer, K.: *CADD - Computer aided database design 1988*
CADD - Computer aided database design. In: Angewandte Informatik. No. 11 (1988), pp. 469 - 477.

Knolmayer, G., Myrach, T.: *Tools zur Darstellung und Analyse von Datenmodellen 1990*
Anforderungen an Tools zur Darstellung und Analyse von Datenmodellen. In: HMD - Theorie und Praxis der Wirtschaftsinformatik. 27 (1990), no. 152, pp. 90-102

Krallmann, H., Scholz-Reiter, B.: *CIM-KSA 1990*
CIM-KSA - Eine rechnergestützte Methode für die Planung von CIM-Informations- und Kommunikationssystemen. In: Reuter, A. (ed.): Computergestützte Informations-, Planungs- und Steuerungssysteme im Unternehmen. Offprint from: Reuter, A. (ed.), GI - 20. Jahrestagung II, Informatik-Fachberichte. Vol. 258, Berlin-Heidelberg-New York-et al. 1990, pp. 57 - 66.

Krcmar, H.: *Gestaltung von "Computer-am-Arbeitsplatz"-Systemen 1983*
Gestaltung von Computer-am-Arbeitsplatz-Systemen (Entwicklung von Alternativen und deren Bewertung durch Simulation). Munich 1983.

Krcmar, H.: *Informationssystem-Architekturen 1990*

Bedeutung und Ziele von Informationssystem-Architekturen. In: Wirtschaftsinformatik. 32 (1990), no. 5, pp. 395 - 402.


Krüger, W.: *Grundlagen der Organisationsplanung 1983*

Grundlagen der Organisationsplanung. Gießen 1983.


Krüger, W.: *Organisation der Unternehmung 1984*

Organisation der Unternehmung. Stuttgart-Berlin-Cologne-Mainz 1984.


Kurbel, K., Dornhoff, P.: *Ein Projektmanagementsystem für evolutionäre Softwareentwicklungen 1990*

Ein Projektmanagementsystem für evolutionäre Softwareentwicklungen auf der Basis eines Drei-Ebenen-Modells. In: Reuter, A. (ed.): Computergestützte Informations-, Planungs- und Steuerungssysteme im Unternehmen. Offprint from: Reuter, A. (ed.), GI - 20. Jahrestagung II, Informatik-Fachberichte. Vol. 258, Berlin-Heidelberg-New York-et al. 1990, pp. 67 - 76.


Kurbel, K., Mertens, P., Scheer, A.-W. (eds.): *Interaktive Informations- und Steuerungssysteme 1989*

Interaktive betriebswirtschaftliche Informations- und Kommunikationssysteme. Berlin-New York 1989.


Kurbel, K., Petsch, W.: *A Cooperative Work Environment 1990*

A Cooperative Work Environment for Evolutionary Software Development. In: Gibbs, S., Verrijn-Stuart, A. A. (eds.): Multi-User Interfaces and Applications. North 1990, pp. 115-127.


Langemeyer, J., Gabriel, S.: *Neuzeitliches Babylon 1990*

Neuzeitliches Babylon erschwert Projektarbeit - Strukturierter Methodenverbund kann Kommunikationsprobleme lösen. In: Computerwoche FOCUS 4, 29th June 1990, pp. 24 - 28


Lockemann, P. C., Schmidt, J. W. (eds.): *Datenbank-Handbuch 1987*

Datenbank-Handbuch. Berlin-Heidelberg-New York-et al. 1987.

Lockemann, P. C., Dittrich, K. R.: *Architektur von Datenbanksystemen 1987*
Architektur von Datenbanksystemen. In: Lockemann, P. C., Schmidt, J. W. (eds.): Datenbank-Handbuch. Berlin-Heidelberg-New York-et al. 1987, pp. 85 - 161.

Löffler, H.: *Lokale Netze 1988*
Lokale Netze. Munich 1988.

Martin, J.: *Application Development 1982*
Application Development Without Programmers. Englewood Cliffs 1982.

Martin, J.: *Information Engineering, Design and Construction 1990*
Information Engineering. Vol. III: Design and Construction. Englewood Cliffs 1990.

Martin, J.: *Information Engineering, Introduction 1989*
Information Engineering. Vol. I: Introduction. London-Sydney-Toronto-et al. 1989.

Martin, J.: *Information Engineering, Planning and Analysis 1990*
Information Engineering. Vol. II: Planning and Analysis. London-Sydney-Toronto-et al. 1990.

Mayr, H. C., Dittrich, K. R., Lockemann, P. C.: *Datenbankentwurf 1987*
Datenbankentwurf. In: Lockemann, P. C., Schmidt, J. W. (Eds.): Datenbank-Handbuch. Berlin-Heidelberg-New York-et al. 1987, pp. 481 - 557.

McMenamin, S. M., Palmer, J. F.: *Strukturierte Systemanayse 1988*
Strukturierte Systemanalyse, mit einem Vorwort von Tom DeMarco. Translated by P. Hruschka, Munich-Vienna-London 1988.

Meyer, B.: *Object-oriented Software Construction 1988*
Object-oriented Software Construction. New York-London-Toronto-et al. 1988.

msp (ed.): *MSP EASY 1990*
msp produkte: MSP EASY - Methoden Fact Book für die Anwendungsentwicklung. MANAGER SOFTWARE PRODUCTS GmbH, Pinneberg 1990.

Nerreter, U.: *Zur funktionalen Architektur von verteilten Datenbanken 1983*
Zur funktionalen Architektur von verteilten Datenbanken - Konzepte, Methoden und Beispiele. Dissertation ETH Zurich 1983.

Olle, T. W., Hagelstein, J., MacDonald, I. G., et al.: *Information Systems 1988*
Information Systems Methodologies: a framework for understanding. Wokingham-Reading-Menlo Park-et al. 1988.

Olle, T. W., Sol, H. G., Tully, C. J. (eds.): *Information Systems 1983*
Information Systems Design Methodologies: A Feature Analysis. Proceedings of the IFIP WG 8.1 Working Conference on Feature Analysis of Information Systems Design Methodologies, York, U.K., 5-7 July, 1983, Amsterdam-New York-Oxford-et al. 1983.

Olle, T. W., Verrijn-Stuart, A. A., Bhabuta, L. (eds.): *Information Systems Life Cycle 1988*
Computerized Assistance During The Information Systems Life Cycle, Proceedings of the IFIP WG 8.1 Working Conference on Computerized Assistance during the Information Systems Life Cycle, CRIS 88, Egham, England, 19 - 22 September 1988, Amsterdam-New York-Oxford-et al. 1988.

Ortner, E., Rössner, J., Söllner, B.: *Entwicklung und Verwaltung standardisierter Datenelemente 1990*
Entwicklung und Verwaltung standardisierter Datenelemente. In: Informatik Spektrum. 13 (1990), pp. 17 - 30.

Page-Jones, M.: *The Practical Guide to Structured System Design 1980*
The Practical Guide to Structured System Design. New York 1980.

Peterson, J. L.: *Petri Net Theory and the Modelling of Systems 1981*
Petri Net Theory and the Modelling of Systems. Englewood Cliffs 1981.

Plattner, H.: *Die Entwicklung des Dialogs zwischen Menschen und Computer 1991*
Die Entwicklung des Dialogs zwischen Menschen und Computer - Eine Betrachtung aus der Sicht der betriebswirtschaftlichen Anwendungen. In: Information Management, 6 (1991), no. 2, publication is in press.

Preßmar, D. B., Eggers, S., Reinken, W.: *Interaktive Entwurfsmethode 1989*

Interaktive Entwurfsmethode zur computergestützten Herstellung betriebswirtschaftlicher Anwendungssoftware. In: Kurbel, K., Mertens, P., Scheer, A.-W. (eds.): Interaktive betriebswirtschaftliche Informations- und Kommunikationssysteme. Berlin-New York 1989.


Reisig, W.: *Systementwurf mit Netzen 1985*

Systementwurf mit Netzen - Petrinetze: Statistische Komponenten, dynamisches Verhalten, Stellen, Transitionen. Berlin-Heidelberg-New York 1985.


Reisig, W.: *Petrinetze 1986*

Petrinetze: Eine Einführung. 2nd ed., Berlin-Heidelberg-New York 1986


Reuter, A.: *Sicherheits- und Integritätsbedingungen 1987*

Maßnahmen zur Wahrung von Sicherheits- und Integritätsbedingungen. In: Lockemann, P. C., Schmidt, J. W. (eds.): Datenbank-Handbuch. Berlin-Heidelberg-New York-et al. 1987, pp. 342 - 441.


Reuter, A. (ed.): *Informatik auf dem Weg zum Anwender 1990*

Proceedings zur GI-20th Jahrestagung: Informatik auf dem Weg zum Anwender. Berlin-Heidelberg-New York-et al. 1990.


Rockart, J. F.: *Critical Success Factors 1982*

Current Uses of the Critical Success Factors Process. In: Proceedings of the Fourteenth Annual Conference of the Society for Information Management, 1982, pp. 17 - 21.


Scheer, A.-W.: *Projektsteuerung 1978*

Projektsteuerung. Wiesbaden 1978.


Scheer, A.-W., Zell, M.: *Benutzergerechte Fertigungssteuerung 1989*

Projektsteuerung. Wiesbaden 1978.


Scheer, A.-W.: *Wirtschaftsinformatik 1990*

Wirtschaftsinformatik - Informationssysteme im Industriebetrieb. 3rd ed., Berlin-Heidelberg-New York-et al. 1990.

Scheer, A.-W.: *CIM 1990*

CIM (Computer Integrated Manufacturing) - Der computergesteuerte Industriebetrieb. 4th ed., Berlin-Heidelberg-New York-et al. 1990.

Scheer, A.-W.: *EDV-orientierte Betriebswirtschaftslehre 1990*

EDV-orientierte Betriebswirtschaftslehre. 4th ed., Berlin-Heidelberg-New York-et al. 1990.

Schlageter, G., Stucky, W.: *Datenbanksysteme 1983*

Datenbanksysteme: Konzepte und Modelle. 2nd ed., Stuttgart 1983.

Schmitz, P., Schönlein, A.: *Optimierungsmodelle 1978*

Lineare und linearisierbare Optimierungsmodelle sowie ihre ADV-gestützte Lösung. Braunschweig 1978.

Schönecker, H. G., Nippa, M.: *Gestaltung der Büroarbeit 1987*

Neue Methoden zur Gestaltung der Büroarbeit. Baden-Baden 1987.

Schönecker, H. G., Nippa, M. (eds.): *Computerunterstützte Methoden für das Informationsmanagement 1990*

Computerunterstützte Methoden für das Informationsmanagement. Baden-Baden 1990.

Schönthaler, F.: *INCOME und CASE* 1990*

INCOME und CASE*: Ein Anwendungsentwicklungssystem für die Produktionsautomatisierung. Straubenhardt 1990 (Berichte aus der Software- und Datenbanktechnik. Ed: F. Schönthaler, Report 2, August 1990).

Schreiber, D.: *Einsatz objektorientierter Konzepte 1990*

Einsatz objektorientierter Konzepte beim Datenbankentwurf für betriebliche Anwendungen. Siegen 1990 (Arbeitsberichte des Lehrstuhls Wirtschaftsinformatik der Universität Siegen, no. 3, September 1990, Ed.: Prof. Dr. M. Grauer).

Siemens (ed.): *GRAPES-SD (SINIX) 1989*

GRAPES-SD (SINIX): Grafisches Entwurfssystem - System Design V1.0. Benutzerhandbuch, 1989.

Sikora, H., Steinparz, F. X.: *Computer & Kommunikation 1988*

Computer & Kommunikation, Telekommunikation - Computervernetzung - Kommunikationsarchitektur - PC/Host-Kommunikation. Übersicht, Zusammenhänge und Fallstudien. Munich 1988.


Sloman, M., Kramer, J.: *Verteilte Systeme und Rechnernetze 1988*

Verteilte Systeme und Rechnernetze. Munich-Englewood Cliffs 1988.


Software AG (eds.): *PREDICT CASE Einführung 1988*

PREDICT CASE Einführung. Darmstadt 1988.


Sol, H. G.: *Information Systems Design Methodologies 1983*

A Feature Analysis of Information Systems Design Methodologies: Methodological Considerations. In: Olle, T. W., Sol, H. G., Tully, C. J. (eds.): Information Systems Design Methodologies: A Feature Analysis. Proceedings of the IFIP WG 8.1 Working Conference on Feature Analysis of Information Systems Design Methodologies, York, U.K., 5-7 July, 1983, Amsterdam-New York-Oxford-et al. 1983, pp. 1 - 8.


Sommerville, I.: *Software Engineering 1987*

Software Engineering. Bonn-Reading-Menlo Park-et al. 1987.


Stetter, F.: *Softwaretechnologie 1983*

Softwaretechnologie: Eine Einführung. 2nd ed. Mannheim-Vienna-Zurich 1983


Strunz, H.: *Informations- und Kommunikationssysteme 1990*

Zur Begründung einer Lehre von der Architektur informationsgestützter Informations- und Kommunikationssysteme. In: Wirtschaftsinformatik, 32 (1990), no. 5, pp. 439 - 445.


Stucky, W., Nemeth, T., Schönthaler, F.: *INCOME 1989*

INCOME - Methoden und Werkzeuge zur betrieblichen Anwendungsentwicklung. In: Kurbel, K., Mertens, P., Scheer, A.-W. (eds.): Interaktive betriebswirtschaftliche Informations- und Kommunikationssysteme. Berlin-New York 1989, pp. 187 - 211.


Tannenbaum, A. S.: *Computer Networks 1988*

Computer Networks. Englewood Cliffs 1988.

Vetter, M.: *Strategie der Anwendungssoftware-Entwicklung 1988*

Strategie der Anwendungssoftware-Entwicklung: Planung, Prinzipien, Konzepte. Stuttgart 1988.


Ward, P. T., Mellor, S. J.: *Structured Development for Real-Time Systems 1985*

Structured Development for Real-Time Systems. Vol. 1: Introduction & Tools. Englewood Cliffs-London et al. 1985.


Wedekind, H.: *Datenbanksysteme I 1981*

Datenbanksysteme I: Eine konstruktive Einführung in die Datenverarbeitung in Wirtschaft und Verwaltung. 2nd ed., Mannheim-Vienna-Zurich 1981.


Winter, F., Maag, D.: *AD/Cycle 1990*

AD/Cycle - Verstärkung für SAA?. In: Information Management. 5 (1990), no. 2, pp. 32 - 39.


Zieher, M.: *Kopplung von Rechnernetzen 1989*

Kopplung von Rechnernetzen. In: Informatik-Fachberichte. Vol. IFB217, Berlin-Heidelberg-New York 1989


Zimmermann, P.: *Einsatz objektorientierter Softwaretechnologie im Rechnungswesen 1990*

Einsatz objektorientierter Softwaretechnologie im Rechnungswesen. In: Scheer, A.-W. (ed.): Rechnungswesen und EDV, 11th Saarbrücker Arbeitstagung 1990, Heidelberg 1990, pp. 235 - 264.

# Index

A.-W. Scheer

# Business Process Engineering

**ARIS-Navigator for Reference Models for Industrial Enterprises**

1994. 5 diskettes 3 1/2", Handbook with approx. 100 pp. ISBN 3-540-14511-7

Once the decision has been made to introduce lean management, the task of actually reengineering the organization's business processes will involve months or even years of work and study. This computer-based description of reference models for reengineering business processes affords valuable assistance to researchers, users and students. The software is a supplement to the book "Scheer, A.-W.: Business Process Engineering. Reference Models for Industrial Enterprises". It contains a complete enterprise model. To the business process owner it can serve as a reference model for actual industrial applications. The context-sensitive navigation enhances the student's understanding of the links between industrial business processes. The models are embedded in the proven "Architecture of Integrated Information Systems"

A.-W. Scheer

# Business Process Engineering

**Reference Models for Industrial Enterprises**

2nd, completely rev. and enlarged ed. 1994. XXIV, 770 pp. 580 figs., 26 in colour
ISBN 3-540-58234-7

The book affords researchers, users and students valuable assistance in implementing new organizational concepts through the employment of new information processing techniques. The structure of the book follows the business processes of logistics, product development, information and coordination, and offers detailed examples of how outdated organizational structures can be reengineered. Examples from standard software systems (especially SAP R/3) demonstrate the book's down-to-earth practicality. The book develops in the views of the proven "Architecture of Integrated Information Systems" (ARIS) a comprehensive enterprise model, which serves as a reference model for engineering concrete business processes in industrial enterprises.

Springer

Tm.B4.9.21b

A.-W. Scheer

# CIM Computer Integrated Manufacturing

## Towards the Factory of the Future

3rd rev. and enl. ed. 1994. XV, 303 pp. 155 figs.
ISBN 3-540-57964-8

Computer Integrated Manufacturing (CIM) is the computerized handling of integrated business processes among all different functions in
an enterprise. The consistent application of information technology,
along with modern manufacturing techniques and new organizational
procedures, opens up great potential for speeding up processes.
This book discusses the current state of applications and new
demands arising from the integration principle. It mainly emphasizes
on strategies for realization and implementation based on the author's
concrete experience. The "Y-CIM information management" model is
presented as a procedural method for implementing CIM. The third
edition has been supplemented by up-to-date specified examples of
applied CIM solutions and transfer strategies.

Tm.B4.9.21b